WORSHIP 4.0

AN EMERGING LIFESTYLE

MARK KAMRATH

Worship 4.0: An Emerging Lifestyle

For information contact: info@theSEEjourney.com

Cover design & editing by Michelle Kamrath

ISBN: 978-0692886441

First Edition: May 2017

Contents

Preface

Worship to me is a time of being with my God. It's a time to celebrate and praise Him with exultant thankfulness, adoration, and awe. It can be a time of quietness, just sitting there, being held. It can be a strategic time of downloads, who does He want to be for me right now, what am I to do with Him moving forward, perhaps even where He wants to take me. Sometimes it's a time of alignment, where I just receive, to understand and see what He is doing, then making the choice to move myself to be in alignment with Him and His purposes.

This is where worship can become a lifestyle. Worship is where I can be loved, and *feel* it. It can be an encounter. It's where I can be at peace, protected from all outside influences and forces. It's a stepping into Him and the environment of heaven. It's where there is no sorrow, no tears (except those of joy!), and no frustration. If it's not in heaven, then it's not in worship. It's a time where there is no time. It's a time of purity, simplicity, and joy, just being with Him.

This is my place with Him, my secret, deep place. I find it when I am alone, and quiet. But can we find that place together, each in our own space with Him, yet all together in worship? I believe we can worship in this way, and that we can do it as a community of believers. This may be a new concept, and one which we will explore. Worship 4.0 can be considered an expanded view of worship through time as we see it in the Bible. Let's consider how we can work together to bring this place in heaven, to earth.

We will consider worship in the Bible, to see how we have arrived in this place of deep connection with our heavenly Father. We'll look at the *how* of taking this territory, and holding space for our true worship leader, the Holy Spirit, and, for a moment at least, bringing this heaven, to earth. Then, we'll consider the part we all play, and some practical aspects of living Worship 4.0.

Introduction

Why "Worship 4.0," and what is it? Worship 4.0 is a model that explores four different "types" or "phases" of worship, characterized primarily by man's relationship to God over time. We will consider worship as it changes through these changing relationships. This book is intended to help the worshiper, worship team member, or worship leader enhance their worship experience and move them to a deeper relationship with Him in everyday life.

Worship 1.0 looks at the time from the creation of man and his life in the Garden of Eden, through the fall of Adam and Eve. Worship 2.0 looks at worship from Cain, Able, Abraham and Jacob up until the Mosaic Law period. Worship 3.0 then covers the initial Mosaic law, and continues through Davidic worship, which added personal freedom and creative expression to the Tabernacle and Temple-based worship of that time. Worship 4.0 then picks up with the giving of Holy Spirit on the day of Pentecost, when for the first time, people were able to become children of God with His Spirit within. This is the period we are in now, and in which we see Worship 4.0 as an emerging form of worship.

We will be exploring a number of concepts through our journey toward Worship 4.0, all intended to add to, and not necessarily replace, our current understanding of worship. We'll be offering an expanded model, or a new way of thinking regarding worship. Let's consider worship as hosting His presence. We are not really "going" anywhere, but experiencing the "on earth as it is in heaven" environment right here where we are.

Heaven on earth is not a mystical thing the Lord does (although it can be!). It also can be a deliberate, intentional, declarative act of His sons and daughters. As His children step into the atmosphere of heaven through worship, praise, kindness, and joy, then that atmosphere of heaven surrounds them in the earthly realm they occupy. That is how heaven invades earth.

Each son and each daughter becomes a portal to the heavenly spiritual realm to which they are citizens (Phil. 3:20). It is tangible and can be felt on earth. It is the privilege and responsibility of those who are called His own. For their home and citizenship is of heaven and they carry that citizenship everywhere they go. This concept was a big part of Jesus' prayer to "let your kingdom come."

In worship, we are simply welcoming people home. Imagine one of your sweet family times, perhaps a Thanksgiving get together. When you went home, there was so much that felt familiar: the neighborhood, the house, the smells, the turkey and dressing that only your family would make. Remember how warm and comforting it was, and the sweet fellowship of close relationships. That is like worship; we are going home.

We will also consider worship as an apostolic act. The Greek word *apostolos* was used in ancient Greece to describe a naval force, or group of freighters. [1] Over time, the meaning became to be a naval force sent with a specific mission. Eventually, it meant to represent the leader of such a force. The Roman use of the word was an apostle sent to a conquered nation, to represent the home nation. He would travel with a fleet of ships and carry people and food from the home nation. There were businessmen, chefs, artists (dance, music, art), writers, and all things Roman.

The apostle's mission was not to replace the cultures that were just conquered, but to inculcate the Roman culture into it, so that the King would feel at home when he visited. Literally, the apostle was to establish the environment or atmosphere of the home nation, the home kingdom. Worship 4.0, as an apostolic act, provides the environment of heaven here on earth, at that place and at that time, to host the King. When He comes to fellowship with us, He finds the culture of His home kingdom: heaven.

Worship is about relationship, not about performance. Whether we stand or sit, raise our hands or not, jump and yell or just smile with our eyes closed, our actions have nothing to do with true worship. Sure, those things may happen, and it's great when they do, but in true worship, it's always as a response or expression as to what is going in *inside*, not coming from direction from the outside.

The worship team becomes His agents to create the atmosphere that will host His presence. They take territory and hold space for the Holy Spirit to do His job, and that is to lead people to Jesus and the Father. Holy Spirit is the true Guide, Teacher, and Comforter after all! The team is to be sensitive to Him, partner with Him, and move where He moves, do what He is doing, and say what He wants them to say.

As worshipers, proper identity is crucial to stepping into Worship 4.0. It's all about relationship, and our relationship with Him will be based upon who we think we are. Our proper identity then becomes thinking about ourselves how He thinks of us. We are to hold heaven's view of ourselves, and not the world's view, or even our own, long-held views. Part of our identity will be our new-found intimacy with God, wherein we will worship Him in spirit and in truth.

The nation of Israel took on the identity as inferior victims, ultimately leading to total captivity, being dominated by their enemies. David restored the identity of royalty, of being God's people, strong, free, and blessed. Unless we think of ourselves as God thinks of us, we will never walk in harmony with His purposes for us. In Worship 4.0, we take this territory, allowing the Holy Spirit to teach us and guide us into who we really are in Him.

- We are accepted in the beloved, as sons and daughters (Eph. 1:3-4).

- We have His in-dwelling spirit (Eph. 2:22).

- We have complete and unhindered access to Him (Eph. 2:18).

A close and intimate relationship as the beloved of God is being restored to God's people. The Church is moving more and more into alignment with her true identity as His beloved. We are not victims, we are not lacking any more, for He came to make us free and complete. This territory is HUGE, and something that can be found in worship.

Scripturally, we will consider Worship 4.0 as part of "something better and greater in view for us" ushered in by the work of the cross, as noted in Hebrews.

> Because God had us in mind and had something better and greater in view for us, so that they [*these heroes and heroines of faith*] should not come to perfection apart from us [*before we could join them*]. (Heb. 11:40 AMP)

Worship 4.0 is both emotional and creative. For decades the Church has believed that emotions are bad, part of the worldly "old man." Nothing could be further from the truth, as God created us with them! They are simply territory promised to us by God for our good, and they need to be taken back, put under His rule and His direction. Also, creativity has been systematically removed from our culture, primarily through the educational systems. [3] Some believe that while creativity is "fun," it's not truly beneficial to society, and not "really" needed, or a career track. (For the most part, the arts and creativity has been relegated to the special few, those particularly gifted, but not for everybody.)

The nature of God is creative! What we first learn of Him in Genesis is that He created. We have His nature now and have the ability to be creative. The Holy Spirit is creative, and *loves* creativity. He works in and with the creative mind. Creativity, and healthy emotional living is territory that has been abdicated to the enemy. It needs to be taken back. As we develop emotionally, and creatively in worship, we begin to claim this territory as our own.

> In him we live and move and have our being'; as even some of your own poets have said, "'For we are indeed his offspring." (Acts 17:28)

In all of this we will explore *rest* as the foundation from which all else springs. Resting in Him in all situations and circumstances seems to be a lost art, with the barrage of media, screens, problems, and societal ills. Worship can build a familiarity of our secret place with Him, how to get there, and perhaps more importantly, how to abide there.

We will explore the power of sound throughout the Bible, considering that major moves of God are accompanied by sound. We'll see how this applies in Worship 4.0 to create an atmosphere to hold space for the Holy Spirit to be present with His people at that moment in time.

Above all, and through all of this, Worship 4.0 is a lifestyle, a relationship with God, not just something we do here and there. Worship is living every breath in agreement with God. It's being a living and walking example of heaven on earth. This is how man was intended to live and how he was originally created. Isn't it interesting that in the garden with Adam and Eve, there is no worship mentioned? This wasn't because there wasn't any, but quite the contrary, everything they did was worship to God. It was a lifestyle for them as they walked with Him in the cool of the day. There was no need for the formality of worship, no altar, no church on Sunday, no commandments, (well, there was one!). There was simply no *activity* noted regarding Adam and Eve's worship. There was no tabernacle, no Ark of the Covenant, no temple, no sacrifices required, no Levites to administer them, and no worship songs.

Adam and Eve's worship was the simple truth that they lived and breathed relationship with God and none other. Their lives were worship to Him. We find this level of living once again given to mankind with the coming of the gift of the Holy Spirit, when man could become once again a whole person of body, soul, and spirit, reconciled completely to God.

> Now may the God of peace himself sanctify you completely, and may your whole spirit and soul and body be kept blameless at the coming of our Lord Jesus Christ. (1 Thess. 5:23)

Worship 4.0 is living with Him in everything we do, whether we are at home, family, work, play, or church, we do all in relationship with Him, never straying, aligned with His purposes and will for us. In a very real sense, we carry a sphere of heaven around us. And when people come into that sphere, they experience a bit of heaven, a bit of the atmosphere of heaven. In your sphere, they can feel how God thinks and be treated how God would treat them. Living in this way *is* worship. This is the whole of His intent for worship, that it's a state of *being*, not just a state of *doing*. The phrase "Be all that you can be" has never been truer. The true fulfillment, however, is found in a full and complete relationship with God, as we live our lives as worship to Him.

The Worship 4.0 model is essentially a look at worship through different periods of time, distinguished by significant changes in God's relationship with man, and the way worship was handled in the Bible. These four periods are:

- Adam and Eve (Paradise)

- Able/Cain, Noah, Abraham

- Moses (Tabernacle) and David (Temple)

- Paul (post-Pentecost accomplishments of Christ)

We will see how God worked with His people through these times, culminating with the worship we are enjoying now, having the completed work of Christ and the availability to become a child of God and receive the gift of the Holy Spirit.

In Spirit and in Truth

We may be aware that in John 4:23-24 true worshipers are said to worship "in spirit and in truth," and that God seeks those who do so. Different people have understood this in different ways, most of which involve looking at spirit and truth as two different things. John 17:17 further defines "truth" as God's Word, often noted as His written Word. This view would say that worship involves both the spirit and the mind, the latter in the understanding of scripture. While this is most certainly true, I believe there is a deeper, more holistic meaning to be found.

> God is spirit, and those who worship him must worship in spirit and truth. (John 4:24)

I believe that the term "in spirit and in truth" is the figure of speech Hendidys, as noted in E.W. Bullingers' *"Figures of Speech Used in the Bible."* [2] Bullinger notes that the greek text shows only one preposition, "in spirit and truth," indicating one entity with two meanings. Both would be true. In this usage, worship would be understood as spiritually true, or truly spiritual. Furthermore, Bullinger notes the imperative *"must,"* meaning this statement is not optional! Worship to our God is a spiritual activity, and *must* be spiritual in order to be true worship. God cannot be truly worshiped by physical means. We become spiritual beings when we receive Christ, and it is our spiritual being from which true worship emanates.

A vivid example of what worship is *not* can be found in Matthew, which is a reference to Isaiah.

> This people honors me with their lips, but their heart is far from me; (Matt. 15:8)

> And the Lord said: "Because this people draw near with their mouth and honor me with their lips, while their hearts are far from me, and their fear of me is a commandment taught by men. (Isa. 29:13)

This is very similar to how we are instructed to love God, which would also be another way to understand worship.

> And you shall love the Lord your God with all your heart and with all your soul and with all your mind and with all your strength. (Mark 12:30)

Our worship, our expression of our love for Him, is to be from our *whole* being, heart, soul, mind, and strength. We cannot truly worship by just singing, playing music, shouting, raising hands, or any other physical expression. True worship *must* flow from the inside out; it *must* flow from our spiritual relationship with our God, from our secret place that only we have with Him, from our heart. From that place, we can express our worship in any number of creative ways, including music, art, and movement.

Jesus was giving us a view of things to come, a new approach, or a new model, of worship. No longer will it be trapped in the ceremony of the temple, but rather, will involve our whole being. Worship is to become an intensely personal and spiritual act.

This new worship will be founded on, and spring from, the personal relationship we can now have with God as a result of the work of Jesus Christ in His death and resurrection. There may (will!) be physical expressions of all kinds in our worship of Him, but they will all emerge out of our personal relationship with Him rather than by external means. The physical is an expression of the internal, and always in that order. Right relationship will always lead to right expression, not the other way around. Forced or legislated external actions will never lead to a close and personal relationship with God. If it did, then our relationship would fall into the category of *works* to bring holiness and acceptance, and that simply is not true. It was the work of Jesus Christ that gave us this new relationship as children of God, and our worshipful expression is simply a response to His great grace and mercy in calling us to be His children. Worship then becomes a spiritual response of our whole being, not solely a physical act.

This type of worship is foreshadowed in the Old Testament as well. Let's consider one of the foundational verses pertaining to worship in Psalm 100.

> Enter his gates with thanksgiving, and his courts with praise! Give thanks to him; bless his name! (Ps. 100:4)

Here, the use of "gates" and "courts" is a reference to the architecture of Solomon's Temple. [4]

SOLOMON'S TEMPLE & COURTS

Enter his gates with thanksgiving, and his courts with praise!
Give thanks to him; bless his name!
Psalm 100:4

We see that there are basically three areas; the gates to enter, the court area, and the temple area, that houses the Holy of Holies with the Ark of the Covenant.

Psalm 100:4 refers to the "gates" and the "courts." Figuratively, we are to enter through the gates and into the courts with thanksgiving and praise respectively. These are shown in the following graphic.

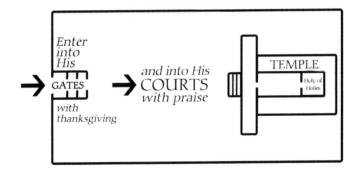

Note the feeling of movement, the flow of the verse when considered in light of the Temple metaphor. Perhaps what speaks most loudly in this verse is what is *not* there, what is missing. Consider the graphic above again, this time allow yourself to feel the flow of the movement represented there. What is missing? Note that the flow moves from the outside to the inside, through the gates and then into the inner courts, but does not make it all the way into the Holy of Holies, the innermost part of the Temple. You can feel that the verse "wants" to go there, but just can't. It's not in the verse.

The Holy of Holies is where the Ark of the Covenant was kept, and in a very real sense, was established as God's presence on earth for this time in history. Sure, God had encounters with people, visiting them from time to time for specific purposes, but the Holy of Holies was considered His "home." This is where the High Priest would go once a year to offer sacrifices for the sins of all the people.

Hebrews speaks in detail about this annual, all-encompassing yet temporary, sacrifice.

> For since the law has but a shadow of the good things to come instead of the true form of these realities, it can never, by the same sacrifices that are continually offered every year, make perfect those who draw near.

Otherwise, would they not have ceased to be offered, since the worshipers, having once been cleansed, would no longer have any consciousness of sins?

But in these sacrifices there is a reminder of sins every year.

For it is impossible for the blood of bulls and goats to take away sins. (Heb. 10:1-4)

Hebrews further explores the role that Jesus played as our High Priest, offering the sacrifice of Himself once and for all for people. He justifies and cleanses all who come to Him.

Consequently, he is able to save to the uttermost those who draw near to God through him, since he always lives to make intercession for them.

For it was indeed fitting that we should have such a high priest, holy, innocent, unstained, separated from sinners, and exalted above the heavens.

He has no need, like those high priests, to offer sacrifices daily, first for his own sins and then for those of the people, since he did this once for all when he offered up himself. (Heb. 7:25-27)

And so, dear brothers and sisters, we can boldly enter heaven's Most Holy Place because of the blood of Jesus.

By His death, Jesus opened a new and life-giving way through the curtain into the Most Holy Place. (Heb. 10:19-20)

The Holy of Holies was the holiest of all places on earth, for it was the place where God lived. Only one man (the High Priest) was ever allowed in there, and that, only once a year. It should also be noted that the opening to the Holy of Holies was covered by a thick woven curtain, estimated to be from one to four inches thick. Both figuratively and literally, Jesus was that one man for us, offering the ultimate sacrifice for us, and breaking down that wall of access allowing us direct access to the presence of God.

> But now in Christ Jesus you who once were far off have been brought near by the blood of Christ.
>
> For he himself is our peace, who has made us both one and has broken down in his flesh the dividing wall of hostility. (Eph. 2:13-14)

The separating wall was broken down, and at the time of Jesus' crucifixion, the thick curtain that separated the Holy of Holies was torn in two, a figurative statement that mankind's access to God was now free and open.

> And behold, the curtain of the temple was torn in two, from top to bottom. And the earth shook, and the rocks were split. (Matt. 27:51)

The Holy of Holies is no longer the place of God's habitation. With the sacrifice of Jesus Christ, and His resurrection, a new dwelling place was instituted. God now dwells within the hearts of all those who receive His Holy Spirit. We now literally have God within us, and we have access to Him every moment of every day. In a very real sense, each one of us is a "Holy of Holies."

> But now in Christ Jesus you who once were far off have been brought near by the blood of Christ.
>
> For he himself is our peace, who has made us both one and has broken down in his flesh the dividing wall of hostility by abolishing the law of commandments expressed in ordinances, that he might create in himself one new man in place of the two, so making peace, and might reconcile us both to God in one body through the cross, thereby killing the hostility.
>
> And he came and preached peace to you who were far off and peace to those who were near.

For through him we both have access in one Spirit to the Father.

So then you are no longer strangers and aliens, but you are fellow citizens with the saints and members of the household of God,

built on the foundation of the apostles and prophets, Christ Jesus himself being the cornerstone, in whom the whole structure, being joined together, grows into a holy temple in the Lord. (Eph. 2:13-21)

In him you also are being built together into a dwelling place for God by the Spirit. (Eph. 2:22)

We literally have Christ *in* us now!

To them God chose to make known how great among the Gentiles are the riches of the glory of this mystery, which is Christ in you, the hope of glory. (Col. 1:27)

So, with that background, let's consider our temple metaphor with respect to worship found in Psalm 100. So what is missing? That final step, that move *into* the Holy of Holies, where we are in the presence of God. Why is it missing? It simply was not available then. It took the coming of God's only begotten Son, and His life, death and resurrection, His complete work of salvation for all, to give us that open access spoken of in Ephesians 2. But look at the beautiful hint Psalm 100 gives us! Through worship we could (in that time and in that way), approach His presence, but never quite get there. For that honor and privilege was reserved for this time in history. It is part of the "better thing" reserved for us spoken of in Hebrews 11, summarized in verses 39 and 40.

And all these, though commended through their faith, did not receive what was promised, since God had provided something better for us, that apart from us they should not be made perfect. (Heb. 11:39-40)

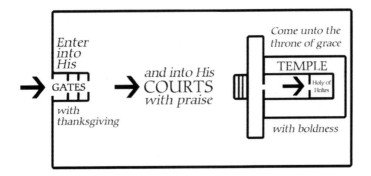

So let's consider Worship 4.0 in light of all this, in light of the completion of what was foreshadowed in Psalm 100, with the following graphic.

Worship 4.0 is that last move into the Holy of Holies. It's abiding in God's presence and living accordingly. But what changed? What gives us that access? I propose that it all comes down to one word: relationship. With the sacrifice and resurrection of Jesus Christ, along with the subsequent giving of Holy Spirit on the day of Pentecost.

> Or do you not know that your body is a temple of the Holy Spirit within you, whom you have from God? You are not your own,
>
> for you were bought with a price. So glorify God in your body. (1 Cor. 6:19-20)

Mankind's relationship with God was re-established once and for all. We became children of God, with all the royal rights and privileges afforded the children of the King. We are now accepted by Him, and beloved by Him.

> The Spirit himself bears witness with our spirit that we are children of God,
>
> and if children, then heirs—heirs of God and fellow heirs with Christ, provided we suffer with him in order that we may also be glorified with him. (Rom. 8:16-17)

Even as he chose us in him before the foundation of the world, that we should be holy and blameless before him. In love. (Eph. 1:4)

The previous graphic shows the movement of worship, with Worship 4.0 being that place of relationship, as beloved sons and daughters of the King, and in His presence. We are told to come into His presence with boldness and confidence because of the work of Jesus, the High Priest for all time.

Since then we have a great high priest who has passed through the heavens, Jesus, the Son of God, let us hold fast our confession.

For we do not have a high priest who is unable to sympathize with our weaknesses, but one who in every respect has been tempted as we are, yet without sin.

Let us then with confidence draw near to the throne of grace, that we may receive mercy and find grace to help in time of need. (Heb. 4:14-16)

Our worship today is a deep and personal celebration of the relationship and access that we have to our God. He seeks those to worship Him this way, truly by the spirit. We can move past prescribed ritual into free expression of our love for Him, which we can only express as we realize His love for us. We are beginning to step into this new worship, the worship that He so deeply desires.

Concepts

As we begin to study the development of worship through time in light of the Worship 4.0 model, we need to consider a few concepts in order to lay a foundation for further understanding.

At, Through, and From the Cross

When considering the things of the Bible, a very important concept to grasp is that some things stopped *at* the cross, some passed *through* the cross, and others began *from* the cross. (The "cross" here represents the whole of the accomplishments of Christ, including his life, death, resurrection, and ascension.) This is a great lens to see things through, especially with the topic of worship. Here are a few quick examples. Blood sacrifices stopped *at* the cross. God's great love for His people, which has been there for all time, passes *through* the cross into now, and being born again of Holy Spirit began *from* the cross. Every biblical truth from Genesis to Revelation can be considered in these terms, and very often can help us with critical understanding of a topic. Imagine if we didn't understand that blood sacrifices ceased *at* the cross with the work of Jesus Christ and His once and for all sacrifice of Himself for all men started there.

This is where we need to understand the *at*, *through*, and *from* the cross concept, as well as the new presence of Holy Spirit within people. It is important to understand that virtually everything about God can be understood in this way.

Here are a few more examples:

> Stopped *at* the cross: Being under the Law (Rom. 6:14)
> Passed *through*: God's love (John 3:16)
> Started *from*: Salvation by grace (Eph. 2:5)

Worship was forever altered by the cross. Some aspects stopped *at* the cross, like animal sacrifices. They were replaced by the one sacrifice of Jesus (Heb. 9:11-12). Some aspects carried *through* the cross, like thanksgiving and praise to God (Heb. 13:15). New aspects of worship started *from* the cross including God's dwelling presence inside His people and their access to Him through the Holy Spirit (2 Cor. 6:16, Eph. 2:18). This in-dwelling presence restored a relationship with God that has been unknown since the garden, but we'll consider that later as we develop the Worship 4.0 model.

The coming and presence of Holy Spirit within each and every individual who is born again is a unique marker of Worship 4.0. With this understanding, we will begin to recognize Worship 4.0 emerging around the world with different groups of people, and in different ways.

Habitation verses Visitation

We live in a habitational culture with God now, not a visitational one. One of the things that started *from* the Cross is that God now dwells *within* His people, not simply "with" them. In worship 2.0, and 3.0, God dwelt with them, for the most part, symbolized by the Ark of the Covenant, and by extension, the Holy of Holies, the innermost part of the Temple. God would visit people at certain times and manifest Himself to them for specific purposes. However, when His people turned from Him, He no longer dwelt with them. It was a visitational culture. Today, God has built us together for a habitation by the Spirit (Ephesians 2:22). We have Christ in us, and the gift of Holy Spirit created within us (Colossians 1:27). No longer does God "visit," He dwells.

This concept determines our mindset when we come to worship. In one case, we are pursuing His presence, inviting Him to come, desperate for Him to come and be with us, assuming of course He isn't there in the first place, and we need Him to "visit" us. In the other, we celebrate that He is already here, with and within us, and we simply enjoy and host His presence. We move from pursing His presence to hosting it. Our attitude is one of partnership and close relationship in rest, rather than feeling alone and desperately hoping He finds us.

Worship as a Place of Being

Consider this concept, and allow it to develop in your heart as we work through this book. I think you'll find that worship *as a place of being* will become a reality for you. Certainly worship, whether individually or with a group, is something we "do." But I propose that the "doing" comes out of the "being." Worship is that secret place that only you and God inhabit, regardless if you are alone, or if there are thousands of people around you, all worshiping too! God is *that* big. He can give his undivided attention to whomever He chooses, however many people there are and wherever they may be.

This secret place is where He can lavish His love and adoration on you. It's where you can sit on His lap, or be held in His arms, or walk in the garden with Him, or pretty much anything else you and He want to do. It's in that place where you can freely and unashamedly offer your love and adoration back to Him, in any form or fashion that you want. You can speak, sing, dance, cry, paint, craft poetry, wave flags, or any other expression you can creatively come up with.

You'll see later that this atmosphere is something that can be created by a worship team, an environment created in the moment to host His presence. Sound has the power to do that, but we'll explore that later as well. For now, let's reframe our understanding of worship as a place wherein we can abide, unique and secret, only us and Him.

Our Responsive Life

It's well known that we can now love, because He first loved us. It's a scripture stated very plainly and easy to be understood. His love for us enables us to both love Him back, and to love others.

We love because He first loved us. (1 John 4:19)

I believe that this is the fundamental pattern of our Christian life, that of responding to what God has already done, or does in the "now" for us. We can of ourselves do nothing (John 5:30), well, of course we "can," but then that wouldn't be responding, would it!

> Not that we are sufficient in ourselves to claim anything as coming from us, but our sufficiency is from God... (2 Cor. 3:5)

We live our life in Him, because of and responding to, the truth that we have been given that life first, by God. Everything from that point forward is to be a response to His goodness, His love, and His working in us.

So, let's apply that responsive life concept to worship. We can only love and adore Him, because He first loved and adored us. He continues to love and adore us. I propose that in order to properly worship, we must first begin to understand how much He loves us, and how much He adores us. This is a concept of identity. We are His beloved!

> To the praise of the glory of his grace, wherein he hath made us accepted in the beloved. (Eph. 1:6 KJV)

We already are accepted. He made us that way in Christ. We are His children, completely, absolutely, complete in Him.

> And ye are complete in him, which is the head of all principality and power: (Col. 2:10)

> By canceling the record of debt that stood against us with its legal demands. This he set aside, nailing it to the cross. (Col. 2:14)

We are complete in Him. Nothing is lacking anymore, for He supplied it on the cross. His resurrection conquered all sin and death. We are no longer "outsiders," but are His beloved, and as the loving Father that He is, He wants only to express that love to us, every day, every moment. This is our identity and how He sees us, and this is the identity we carry into our secret place of worship. In worship, we allow Him to love us and show us His affection toward us, then we live and worship *from* that place, not *toward* it. We don't worship in order to garner His attention, or His affection. He *already* offers it! You see, this is a place of *being*, not *doing*.

Worship is a place to abide, a place of being overwhelmed with how He sees us, and how He thinks of us. From this place, we respond, worship creatively, and move out in life responding to His goodness and kindness.

The Importance of Rest

The importance of rest and its role in worship cannot be overstated. Rest itself is a place of being, not a lack (or avoidance) of activity. We will see through scriptural development that the biblical concept of "rest" is quite different from common understanding. Actually, we can undertake any activity from a place of rest, and be supremely productive. Let's see what we can discover regarding rest in the Bible.

As mentioned before, worship and the Old Testament activities of worship were not mentioned in the original paradise, mostly because they simply were not needed. There was no need for sacrifices to atone for man's sin, as sin had not happened yet. Man had all authority under God, and next to walking with God in the cool of the day, his primary job was to tend the garden. These responsibilities in the garden, "to work it and keep it," seemed to be a very peaceful and restful existence for Adam and Eve. Still, they did sin, and disobeyed God. At this point, many things happened to the relationship between God and man, (too many for a thorough consideration here), but there are a few consequences that are important to consider with regard to rest and worship.

Also, we will consider rest in the context of work, with work being the effort, or offering, of our own hands, in opposition of resting in the work of God's hands. We will see the common thread through all time of the futility of our own work, and the need to rest in God's work that He accomplished for us.

Adam and Eve

The concept of hard work, resulting in "sweat" was introduced with the fall of man. Sweat was not mentioned in the original garden paradise. A consideration of the early Genesis record of the fall of man will show that the disobedience of Eve, and later Adam, to a direct commandment of God was due to their desire to "do," rather than simply "be." They were deceived into thinking God was not doing enough for them and they were missing something, so they needed to "do" something on their own in order to get all they should have. So *they* ate from the forbidden fruit; it was *their* decision and *their* action.

> And unto Adam he said, Because thou hast hearkened unto the voice of thy wife, and hast eaten of the tree, of which I commanded thee, saying, Thou shalt not eat of it: cursed is the ground for thy sake; in sorrow shalt thou eat of it all the days of thy life;
>
> Thorns also and thistles shall it bring forth to thee; and thou shalt eat the herb of the field;
>
> In the sweat of thy face shalt thou eat bread, till thou return unto the ground; for out of it wast thou taken: for dust thou *art*, and unto dust shalt thou return.
>
> And Adam called his wife's name Eve; because she was the mother of all living.
>
> Unto Adam also and to his wife did the LORD God make coats of skins, and clothed them. (Gen. 3:17-21)

"Sweat" is only mentioned three times in Bible. This is the first occurrence in verse 19 of Genesis 3, where Adam and Eve were told that from this point forward they, and mankind in general, would need to work hard to raise food, so much so it would result in "the sweat of thy face." Could it be that the cursed ground and additional thorns and thistles made it more difficult?

The other two times "sweat" occurs are in Ezekiel, when describing what the Levites could wear and when Jesus was praying in the garden before His Crucifixion. We'll consider both of these later in our study of rest.

Cain and Able

The consideration of the sacrifices of both Cain and Able also shows us the difference between the work of our own hands, and resting in the works of God.

> And in process of time it came to pass, that Cain brought of the fruit of the ground an offering unto the LORD.
>
> And Abel, he also brought of the firstlings of his flock and of the fat thereof. And the LORD had respect unto Abel and to his offering:
>
> But unto Cain and to his offering he had not respect. And Cain was very wroth, and his countenance fell. (Gen. 4:3-5)

Lets consider the difference between these two offerings. At the time of man's fall from the garden, Adam and Eve sought leaves to "cover" themselves. This was more than just clothing, but symbolic of man's need to work to cover their own sin.

> Then the eyes of both were opened, and they knew that they were naked. And they sewed fig leaves together and made themselves loincloths. (Gen. 3:7)

God saw this and provided animal skins for their covering, thereby offering His works (Gen. 3:21). It is also significant that in order to get animal skins, blood must be shed, and Leviticus 16:15 shows us that blood is required for a sin offering. We see later in Hebrews that without the shedding of blood, there is no payment for sin.

> Indeed, under the law almost everything is purified with blood, and without the shedding of blood there is no forgiveness of sins. (Heb. 9:22)

Furthermore, the blood sacrifices of the Old Testament are foreshadowing the sacrifice of Jesus Christ, once and for all, for our sin. So in consideration of the offerings of Cain and Able,

Cain offered the fruit of the ground, which was cursed and Able offered the firstlings of his flock. The fruit offering may have seemed like a good idea, but it was not what God had set up as the payment for sin. Able's offering of the firstlings of his flock was in keeping with the necessity of shed blood to cover sin. So Cain did it his way, and Able did it God's way. Doing things "God's way" is resting in His work.

Moses (Tabernacle)

When God told Moses to take the children of Israel into the promised land, Moses had an honest discussion with the Lord.

> Moses said to the LORD, "See, you say to me, 'Bring up this people,' but you have not let me know whom you will send with me. Yet you have said, 'I know you by name, and you have also found favor in my sight.'
>
> Now therefore, if I have found favor in your sight, please show me now your ways, that I may know you in order to find favor in your sight. Consider too that this nation is your people."
>
> And he said, "My presence will go with you, and I will give you rest."
>
> And he said to him, "If your presence will not go with me, do not bring us up from here. (Exod. 33:12-15)

In the presence of the Lord there is rest. Moses was not willing to travel into unknown territory unless the presence of God was with him. Earlier, when Moses was instructed to build the Tabernacle, he was not to use "hewn stone," for that would have required the work of man.

> And the LORD said unto Moses, Thus thou shalt say unto the children of Israel, Ye have seen that I have talked with you from heaven. (Exod. 20:22)

> And if thou wilt make me an altar of stone, thou shalt not build it of hewn stone: for if thou lift up thy tool upon it, thou hast polluted it. (Exod. 20:25)

Here, the "work" done was to be God's work of natural stone, and not man's. This concept of resting in God's work, and not man's, is critical to our study of worship. In Numbers, the children of Israel were in the wilderness and quarreled with Moses because they were thirsty. When Moses asked the Lord what to do, He gave specific instructions.

> "Take the staff, and assemble the congregation, you and Aaron your brother, and tell the rock before their eyes to yield its water. So you shall bring water out of the rock for them and give drink to the congregation and their cattle"...
>
> And Moses and Aaron gathered the congregation together before the rock, and he said unto them, Hear now, ye rebels; must we fetch you water out of this rock?
>
> And Moses lifted up his hand, and with his rod he smote the rock twice: and the water came out abundantly, and the congregation drank, and their beasts *also.*
>
> And the LORD spake unto Moses and Aaron, Because ye believed me not, to sanctify me in the eyes of the children of Israel, therefore ye shall not bring this congregation into the land which I have given them. (Num. 20:8, 10-12)

Moses performed a miracle that day and yet the Lord said, "ye believed me not, to sanctify me..." He was to "sanctify" God in the eyes of Israel that day, but he didn't. Moses complained "must *we* fetch you water," showing himself and Aaron as the providers. Because of this He and Aaron were not allowed to enter the promised land. He made it about his work, rather than the true "Rock" the Lord Jesus as stated in first Corinthians.

> And were all baptized unto Moses in the cloud and
> in the sea;
>
> And did all eat the same spiritual meat;
>
> And did all drink the same spiritual drink: for they
> drank of that spiritual Rock that followed them:
> and that Rock was Christ. (1 Cor. 10:2-4)

The rock that Moses hit symbolized the true source of
provision and sustenance: Christ. It was in Christ that Moses
needed to rest, but in this incident, he took the task upon himself
instead. Taking on the work as Israel's provider was a mistake so
crucial, that this disobedience kept him and Aaron from going
into the promised land.

Joshua

When the children of Israel were about to go into the promised
land the first time, Moses sent out ten men to spy out the land
to see who and what was there. Eight returned saying, "We be
not able to go up against the people; for they are stronger than
we." (Num. 13:31) Two men, Joshua and Caleb brought back
the report that, "If the LORD delights in us, he will bring us into
this land and give it to us..." (Num. 14:8)

Eight spies looked at man's ability and two rested in God's.
Because of this the Lord told Moses that none of these people,
except Joshua and Caleb, "shall see the land that I swore to give
to their fathers. And none of those who despised me shall see it."
(Num 14:23). Israel was prevented from entering the promised
land and had to wander in the wilderness 40 years until they all
died off. The next generation was allowed to go in.

> When your fathers tempted me, proved me, and
> saw my works forty years.
>
> Wherefore I was grieved with that generation, and
> said, They do alway err in their heart; and they
> have not known my ways.

> So I sware in my wrath, They shall not enter into
> my rest.) (Heb. 3:9-11)

After Moses and that generation died, Joshua led the nation of Israel into the land with these words, "The LORD your God is providing you a place of rest and will give you this land." (Joshua 1:13). God performed supernatural acts in order for Israel to conquer the land and at the end of it all, it is recorded:

> Thus the LORD gave to Israel all the land that he swore to give to their fathers. And they took possession of it, and they settled there.
>
> And the LORD gave them rest on every side just as he had sworn to their fathers. Not one of all their enemies had withstood them, for the LORD had given all their enemies into their hands.
>
> Not one word of all the good promises that the LORD had made to the house of Israel had failed; all came to pass. (Joshua 21:43-45)

David (Solomon's Temple)

When Solomon, David's son, was building the Temple, the workers were instructed to perform all tool-related construction off-site, then assemble on-site, so as not to have the sound of work anywhere near the area.

> When the house was built, it was with stone prepared at the quarry, so that neither hammer nor axe nor any tool of iron was heard in the house while it was being built. (1 Kings 6:7)

The Temple represented Christ in an architectural art form, and it was to represent His work, not man's. The sound of the tools represented the work of man, and even the sound of work was not allowed.

In Genesis, the word "sweat" represented man's work. It is used for a second time in regard to the Levites' service in the

Temple. In Ezekiel, the priests were instructed to only wear linen, so *not* to sweat.

> When they enter the gates of the inner court, they shall wear linen garments. They shall have nothing of wool on them, while they minister at the gates of the inner court, and within.
>
> They shall have linen turbans on their heads, and linen undergarments around their waists. They shall not bind themselves with anything that causes sweat. (Ezek. 44:17-18)

The aspect of sweating could not be part of their worship, just as the sound of work was not heard while the Temple was being built. I believe this is a physical characteristic that represents a spiritual reality. *Sweat* represents man's work, and man's work has no place in the worship of God.

Christ

The third reference to *sweat* is found in Luke. Jesus was completing His work by offering Himself on the cross, a horrendously painful way to die, as the sacrifice for mankind. Before he is led to the cross, he is found praying in a garden.

> And being in agony he prayed more earnestly; and his sweat became like great drops of blood falling down to the ground. (Luke 22:44)

Jesus' *sweat*, described as "blood," was His redemptive work when He gave His blood for mankind. It was the work of Christ, His sweat, that was "falling down to the ground." It soaked the same ground that was cursed because of Adam's disobedience.

In the writings of Paul's time, we see that we must rest in this finished work of Christ.

> So then, there remains a Sabbath rest for the people of God,

for whoever has entered God's rest has also rested from his works as God did from his.

Let us therefore strive to enter that rest, so that no one may fall by the same sort of disobedience. (Heb. 4:8-11)

It says to "strive to enter that rest." Our work is to rest in *His* work! We are His workmanship and it is by His work that we are saved. Just as in the Old Testament, it is not about our works or man's provision, it is about His work and His provision.

For by grace you have been saved through faith. And this is not your own doing; it is the gift of God,

Not a result of works, so that no one may boast. (Eph. 2:9-10)

...worship God in the spirit, and rejoice in Christ Jesus, and have no confidence in the flesh. (Phil. 3:3)

Our worship must be "in the spirit," and be based on what Christ accomplished, not on our flesh, our own work, or what we are able to do. It becomes a lifestyle of living in Christ and is present in everything we do.

Summary

Rest is not an absence of activity, but a place of empowerment, peace, and purpose. It's a state of being wherein you are fully engaged with the purposes of God in your life, living your responsive life doing what He is doing. Rest is that place you find the real you, and where you see yourself as God sees you, holy and beloved of Him. It's your secret place with Him where you can go and simply "be," be His.

Rest is intended to be a lifestyle, and can be found in worship together with your community in Christ. Your community worship can be that place where you discover and build your relationship with God, so that it begins to become more and more your lifestyle, your way of thinking, and your way of operating.

Throughout the Bible, the Temple was the place of worship and represented Christ. Because of this it was not allowed to be built with the sound of work near it. The Levites were not allowed to sweat while they ministered and worshipped in it. This is a picture of our worship in spirit and in truth, where we enter in the rest and confidence of what the Lord Jesus accomplished with His blood. We will need to work to enter the rest of God so that we rest in what He has done, not in our own works. In His rest, thanksgiving and worship are a part of everything we do.

The Power of Sound

In this section we will consider numerous examples of the power that sound exhibited in an number of contexts.

I believe that sound can penetrate barriers otherwise impenetrable. It can penetrate areas of the heart otherwise closed off. The power of sound, spoken, sung, or made through instruments, has the ability to sneak past the guard, slide under the gate, jump the wall, and be lowered into the caverns. It is the one thing that travels freely from place to place unhindered.

The Ancient Hebrew symbols for "sound" are ᒐ-•. [5] Reading from right to left, the first symbol is the sun on the horizon, which literally means the gathering of the light. The second symbol is the shepherds staff, and carries the meaning of authority, or more specifically, a gathering to the shepherd's voice. The combination of these symbols applied to the word "sound" is very interesting. It literally means sound is a gathering of light, calling one to the voice of the shepherd. "Light" here is a positive place, and the shepherd is one who provides, protects, and directs. In the context of worship, that shepherd would be our God. But there are many usages of the word "sound" in the Bible, all of which carry this same root meaning.

We will consider the following contexts in our exploration of the power of sound:

1. Sound as a creative force

2. Sound as power to take territory

3. Sound in warfare

4. Sound as the presence of God

5. Sound that ushers in the presence of God

Sound as a Creative Force

God is the great Creator, and we can see the power of sound evidenced in the creation record of Genesis. In Genesis 1:3 it says, "And God said... " Here we see the record of the actual creation of all we know now. Note that God is the power behind the creation, and two aspects are noted here in Genesis. One is words. God used words to create, which also speaks to the power and creativity of words themselves. But often overlooked is the word "said." It doesn't say "think"! In order to "say" something, a sound must be produced. The sound spoken of here carried God's words of creation. So even in the original creation, sound carried the power of the words, the power of all creation itself.

Sound has long been described as waves of pressure, a force that has the ability to move objects or cause physical damage. There is even a branch of science, called Cymatics, that studies patterns made by sound with sand on a metal plate, or in liquid. Further information could be found in a web article "Seeing the Patterns in Sound," found at sciencefriday.com [6].

The Taking of Territory

Sound is often mentioned in records of warfare and the taking of territory. In particular, David's taking of territory shows God's redemptive power as He worked with David to restore all that was promised to the nation of Israel earlier.

God uses sound to bring about deliverance for Moses and his people in these scriptures.

> And when you go to war in your land against the adversary who oppresses you, then you shall sound an alarm with the trumpets, that you may be remembered before the LORD your God, and you shall be saved from your enemies. (Num. 10:9)

This is the familiar account of the walls of Jericho. There were a number of factors that contributed to Joshuas' victory here, including obedience to God's instructions, faithfulness, and patience. But also noted was a great sound of shouting and trumpets.

> And when they make a long blast with the ram's horn, when you hear the sound of the trumpet, then all the people shall shout with a great shout, and the wall of the city will fall down flat, and the people shall go up, everyone straight before him." (Josh. 6:5)

Samuel found that God provided a victory for him by bringing a thundering mighty sound, and a sound of marching in the following accounts.

> As Samuel was offering up the burnt offering, the Philistines drew near to attack Israel. But the LORD thundered with a mighty sound that day against the Philistines and threw them into confusion, and they were routed before Israel. (1 Sam. 7:10)

> And when you hear the sound of marching in the tops of the balsam trees, then rouse yourself, for then the LORD has gone out before you to strike down the army of the Philistines." (2 Sam. 5:24)

Musicians Lead the Army

This is an interesting account where Jehoshaphat looked to God for direction regarding an upcoming battle. Armies had come against Israel, and Jehoshaphat encouraged the people to believe in God and the prophets, or more specifically, what the prophets said.

> And they rose early in the morning and went out into the wilderness of Tekoa. And when they went out, Jehoshaphat stood and said, "Hear me, Judah and inhabitants of Jerusalem! Believe in the LORD your God, and you will be established; believe his prophets, and you will succeed."

> And when he had taken counsel with the people, he appointed those who were to sing to the LORD and praise him in holy attire, as they went before the army, and say, "Give thanks to the LORD, for his steadfast love endures forever."
>
> And when they began to sing and praise, the LORD set an ambush against the men of Ammon, Moab, and Mount Seir, who had come against Judah, so that they were routed. (2 Chron. 20:20-22)

This is such a great account! Faced with impending destruction, the people gave thanks to God, and celebrated His love. In response, God orchestrated an ambush that provided the victory. Note specifically that when they began to sing and praise (music and voices), the victory was accomplished. Sound produced from obedient hearts, is indeed a very powerful reality.

Musical Sound as Praise

There are many examples of sound being used to praise God. We just saw one in the previous section, in 2 Chronicles 20. Following are accounts of sound produced by both instruments and voices being used to praise God.

> 4,000 gatekeepers, and 4,000 shall offer praises to the LORD with the instruments that I have made for praise." (1 Chron. 23:5)
>
> Raise a song; sound the tambourine, the sweet lyre with the harp. (Ps. 81:2)
>
> Sing praises to the LORD with the lyre, with the lyre and the sound of melody!
>
> With trumpets and the sound of the horn make a joyful noise before the King, the LORD! (Ps. 98:5-6)

> Praise him with trumpet sound; praise him with
> lute and harp! (Ps. 150:3)

Sound as the Presence of God

With rumblings at the top of a mountain, trumpets, a roar of many waters, and even a quiet whisper, the presence of God has been noted by sound. Music was even shown to set an atmosphere of heaven so that people would receive words from God. In the account of Moses interacting with God on the mountain, very loud sounds accompanied God's presence.

> On the morning of the third day there were thunders and lightnings and a thick cloud on the mountain and a very loud trumpet blast, so that all the people in the camp trembled.
>
> Then Moses brought the people out of the camp to meet God, and they took their stand at the foot of the mountain.
>
> And as the sound of the trumpet grew louder and louder, Moses spoke, and God answered him in thunder. (Exod. 19:16-17, 19)

In the following account, the prophet Elijah was being pursued by Jezebel, and was on the run in Beersheba. From there, he went out into the wilderness to have a chat with God about the whole thing, and life in general.

> There he came to a cave and lodged in it. And behold, the word of the LORD came to him, and he said to him, "What are you doing here, Elijah?"
>
> He said, "I have been very jealous for the LORD, the God of hosts. For the people of Israel have forsaken your covenant, thrown down your altars, and killed your prophets with the sword, and I, even I only, am left, and they seek my life, to take it away."

And he said, "Go out and stand on the mount before the LORD." And behold, the LORD passed by, and a great and strong wind tore the mountains and broke in pieces the rocks before the LORD, but the LORD was not in the wind. And after the wind an earthquake, but the LORD was not in the earthquake.

And after the earthquake a fire, but the LORD was not in the fire. And after the fire the sound of a low whisper.

And when Elijah heard it, he wrapped his face in his cloak and went out and stood at the entrance of the cave. And behold, there came a voice to him and said, "What are you doing here, Elijah?" (1 Kings 19:9-13)

God indeed has a "voice" that is a sound.

Hear attentively the noise of his voice, and the sound *that* goeth out of his mouth. (Job 37:2)

There are also numerous references of sound in heaven.

And under the expanse their wings were stretched out straight, one toward another. And each creature had two wings covering its body.

And when they went, I heard the sound of their wings like the sound of many waters, like the sound of the Almighty, a sound of tumult like the sound of an army. When they stood still, they let down their wings. (Ezek. 1:23-24)

And behold, the glory of the God of Israel was coming from the east. And the sound of his coming was like the sound of many waters, and the earth shone with his glory. (Ezek. 43:2)

And I heard a voice from heaven like the roar of many waters and like the sound of loud thunder.

The voice I heard was like the sound of harpists playing on their harps, (Rev. 14:2)

Sound that Ushers in the Presence of God

Sound can spiritually bring refreshing or destruction. The key resides in the heart of the one making or producing the sound. Scripture seems to imply that the heart of the one producing the sound is spiritually carried on the waves of the sound. When a heart is in harmony with heaven, the sound that is produced ushers in an atmosphere of heaven. It carries with it the heart that produces it. The heart has the ability to direct and affect the environment in which it is placed and the sound from the heart shapes and molds that environment. Sound is something that can usher in an environment.

Samuel instructed Saul early in his ministry to seek out a group of prophets, who were prophesying with music.

> After that you shall come to Gibeath-elohim, where there is a garrison of the Philistines. And there, as soon as you come to the city, you will meet a group of prophets coming down from the high place with harp, tambourine, flute, and lyre before them, prophesying.
>
> Then the Spirit of the LORD will rush upon you, and you will prophesy with them and be turned into another man. (1 Sam. 10:5-6)

This shows that music played by the prophets, as well as their voices "prophesying," ushered in the presence of the Lord upon Saul. Later, when Saul had turned away from the Lord, evil spirits would come upon him. It was at that time that the young David became King Saul's armor-bearer. David had already been anointed by Samuel and had God's favor upon him. Whenever David played his lyre, the evil spirits who were on Saul would leave him. They could not occupy the same space and they had to go. This shows that the music David played carried with it a powerful spiritual dimension. It carried God's favor that was on David, into the room.

> And David came to Saul and entered his service. And Saul loved him greatly, and he became his armor-bearer.
>
> And Saul sent to Jesse, saying, "Let David remain in my service, for he has found favor in my sight."
>
> And whenever the harmful spirit from God was upon Saul, David took the lyre and played it with his hand. So Saul was refreshed and was well, and the harmful spirit departed from him. (1 Sam. 16:21-23)

Music was also part of transporting the Ark of the Covenant into Jerusalem by David. As noted before, the Ark not only represented, but actually hosted the presence of God. You'll see that when the Ark was placed in the temple, God's presence filled the rooms, accompanied with all sorts of music.

> So all Israel brought up the ark of the covenant of the LORD with shouting, to the sound of the horn, trumpets, and cymbals, and made loud music on harps and lyres. (1 Chron. 15:28)
>
> So David and all the house of Israel brought up the ark of the LORD with shouting, and with the sound of the trumpet. (2 Sam. 6:15)
>
> and it was the duty of the trumpeters and singers to make themselves heard in unison in praise and thanksgiving to the LORD), and when the song was raised, with trumpets and cymbals and other musical instruments, in praise to the LORD, "For he is good, for his steadfast love endures forever," the house, the house of the LORD, was filled with a cloud,   (2 Chron. 5:13)

When Jehoshaphat, the King of Israel, asked for God's insight from the prophet Elisha, the prophet requested that a musician be brought so that he would receive a word from the Lord.

> And Jehoshaphat said, "The word of the LORD is
> with him." So the king of Israel and Jehoshaphat
> and the king of Edom went down to him.
>
> And Elisha said to the king of Israel, "What have I
> to do with you? Go to the prophets of your father
> and to the prophets of your mother." But the king
> of Israel said to him, "No; it is the LORD who has
> called these three kings to give them into the hand
> of Moab."
>
> And Elisha said, "As the LORD of hosts lives... But
> now bring me a musician." And when the musician
> played, the hand of the LORD came upon him. (2
> Kings 3:12-15)

Sound ushered in the birth of the Lord Jesus as humble
shepherds in their field witnessed God's announcement. It came
with heavenly worship and words from a heavenly host.

> And suddenly there was with the angel a multitude
> of the heavenly host praising God and saying,
>
> "Glory to God in the highest, and on earth peace
> among those with whom he is pleased!" (Luke
> 2:13-14)

In the New Testament, the coming of the Holy Spirit in Acts
was accompanied with sound.

> And suddenly there came from heaven a sound
> like a mighty rushing wind, and it filled the entire
> house where they were sitting. (Acts 2:2)

Just as sound was part of the first coming, so it will usher
in the second coming of the Lord. He will come with the cry of
command from an archangel and the trumpet of God.

> For the Lord himself will descend from heaven with
> a cry of command, with the voice of an archangel,
> and with the sound of the trumpet of God. And
> the dead in Christ will rise first. (1 Thess. 4:16)

There is a spiritual power of sound that is evidenced in the physical. God designed the world this way, and our lives can benefit from all He has given us in the power of sound. As we move forward into the consideration of the Worship 4.0 model, we'll see that sound plays a crucial part in both establishing and holding space for the Holy Spirit to do His work in our worship services. Sound will play a powerful part in bringing this portal of heaven to earth.

I believe that these aspects of creativity, the taking of territory, and of God's presence are all contained in the power of sound in worship. We may not be capturing land, but we are to take the territory of people's hearts, emotions, and thoughts. Worship can provide that atmosphere, hold that space for God to work and this brings us to the consideration of Worship 4.0 in greater detail.

Worship 1.0

As we begin our consideration of worship through time, let's review the 4.0 model. The phases of worship, 1.0 through 4.0, are periods of time, each distinguished by unique and specific aspects of God's relationship to man. You will see that there is an evolution of expression, relationship, and roles all leading to this wonderful time we call our "now."

Worship 1.0 covers the time from the creation of man and woman to their subsequent expulsion from the garden. This is a very short record in the Bible, but there is much to be learned from it.

> The LORD God took the man and put him in the garden of Eden to work it and keep it.
>
> And the LORD God commanded the man, saying, "You may surely eat of every tree of the garden,
>
> but of the tree of the knowledge of good and evil you shall not eat, for in the day that you eat of it you shall surely die."
>
> Then the LORD God said, "It is not good that the man should be alone; I will make him a helper fit for him." (Genesis 2:15-18)

Let's consider these sections in light of the relationship God had with Adam and Eve. First, we see that God gave Adam a job. He was to keep the garden of Eden, and work it. Was man created with this knowledge? Perhaps he needed God's help, and needed to talk to Him in order to learn how to perform this task.

We also see the one commandment they were to keep. Scripture indicates this commandment was communicated with conversation. They were talking together, and God said "Hey Adam, you have all this cool stuff you can do, but don't do this one thing. If you do, it won't work out so good for you." Or words to that effect!

This next part is really interesting. God asked Adam to name every creature God had created earlier. Now, Adam didn't have a thesaurus, or reference library with which to confer. God genuinely wanted to know what Adam would call them, as a partner in creativity!

> Now out of the ground the LORD God had formed every beast of the field and every bird of the heavens and brought them to the man to see what he would call them. And whatever the man called every living creature, that was its name.
>
> The man gave names to all livestock and to the birds of the heavens and to every beast of the field...

God brought him an animal, and said "What do you want to call this one?" Then Adam would say "somethin' somethin'," and the animal had a name. God could easily have named them by Himself, then given Adam a book with pictures with all the names, and called it a day, but God *wanted* to partner with Adam. He *wanted* to fellowship and co-create with him.

> ...But for Adam there was not found a helper fit for him.
>
> So the LORD God caused a deep sleep to fall upon the man, and while he slept took one of his ribs and closed up its place with flesh.
>
> And the rib that the LORD God had taken from the man he made into a woman and brought her to the man.
>
> Then the man said, "This at last is bone of my bones and flesh of my flesh; she shall be called Woman, because she was taken out of Man."
>
> Therefore a man shall leave his father and his mother and hold fast to his wife, and they shall become one flesh.

And the man and his wife were both naked and were not ashamed. (Gen. 2:15-25)

And they heard the sound of the LORD God walking in the garden in the cool of the day, and the man and his wife hid themselves from the presence of the LORD God among the trees of the garden.

But the LORD God called to the man and said to him, "Where are you?"

And he said, "I heard the sound of you in the garden, and I was afraid, because I was naked, and I hid myself."

He said, "Who told you that you were naked? Have you eaten of the tree of which I commanded you not to eat?" (Gen. 3:8-11)

In Genesis chapter three, after they ate the fruit, but before they were kicked out of the garden, we see God having a difficult conversation with Adam and Eve. They were conversing, as they usually did. Verse eight notes that they "heard" the sound of the Lord God walking. This is what they did and was part of their daily routine. They walked with their God in the cool of the day.

These passages are indicative of the relationship God originally had with man. God wanted to work with him, be friends with him, partner with him, talk to him, and create with him. In doing all of this, Adam and Eve lived in alignment with God and His purposes. This I believe is the original model for worship. Life with God, a pure, close, and intimate relationship with the God of the heavens.

KEY ASPECT: Adam and Eve has a personal, intimate relationship with God where they were friends with Him, walked with Him, and talked with Him.

KEY ASPECT: Adam and Eve were partners with God, co-creating the paradise they were living in.

Worship 2.0

Worship 2.0 covers the time from man's expulsion from the garden up to the point where Moses received the Law and began to build the Tabernacle, as instructed by God. The first reference to worship in this time frame is in Genesis four, and simply refers to "offerings."

> And in process of time it came to pass, that Cain brought of the fruit of the ground an offering unto the LORD.
>
> And Abel, he also brought of the firstlings of his flock and of the fat thereof. And the LORD had respect unto Abel and to his offering:
>
> But unto Cain and to his offering he had not respect. And Cain was very wroth, and his countenance fell. (Gen. 4:3-5)

Offerings and alters are the hallmark of Worship 2.0. There were no elaborate rituals or edifices, just simple offerings. The previous verses mentioned Cain and Abel, but Noah and Abraham built altars as well.

> Then Noah built an altar to the LORD and took some of every clean animal and some of every clean bird and offered burnt offerings on the altar. (Gen. 8:20)
>
> Then the LORD appeared to Abram and said, "To your offspring I will give this land." So he built there an altar to the LORD, who had appeared to him.
>
> From there he moved to the hill country on the east of Bethel and pitched his tent, with Bethel on the west and Ai on the east. And there he built an altar to the LORD and called upon the name of the LORD. (Gen. 12:7-8)

> to the place where he had made an altar at the
> first. And there Abram called upon the name of
> the LORD. (Gen. 13:4)

> So Abram moved his tent and came and settled
> by the oaks of Mamre, which are at Hebron, and
> there he built an altar to the LORD. (Gen. 13:18)

Abraham, Jacob's father, built a total of four altars in his life. They were all built to acknowledge and worship God. Jacob followed in his father's footsteps and continued to build altars with which to worship God in the offering of sacrifices.

> God said to Jacob, "Arise, go up to Bethel and dwell
> there. Make an altar there to the God who appeared
> to you when you fled from your brother Esau."

> So Jacob said to his household and to all who
> were with him, "Put away the foreign gods that
> are among you and purify yourselves and change
> your garments.

> Then let us arise and go up to Bethel, so that I may
> make there an altar to the God who answers me
> in the day of my distress and has been with me
> wherever I have gone." (Gen. 35:1-3)

Later there is an interesting account of God appearing to Jacob, giving him a prophetic promise. It is interesting to note that Jacob's response was to build a quick altar and offer sacrifices.

> God appeared to Jacob again, when he came from
> Paddan-aram, and blessed him.

> And God said to him, "Your name is Jacob; no
> longer shall your name be called Jacob, but Israel
> shall be your name." So he called his name Israel.

> And God said to him, "I am God Almighty: be
> fruitful and multiply. A nation and a company
> of nations shall come from you, and kings shall
> come from your own body.

The land that I gave to Abraham and Isaac I will give to you, and I will give the land to your offspring after you."

Then God went up from him in the place where he had spoken with him.

And Jacob set up a pillar in the place where he had spoken with him, a pillar of stone. He poured out a drink offering on it and poured oil on it.

So Jacob called the name of the place where God had spoken with him Bethel. (Gen. 35:9-15)

Note that Jacob did not build a formal altar this time but rather, a pillar of stone, upon which he offered drink and oil. This is quite an artistic expression, both physically and metaphorically with his offering! Also, notice that Jacob's response to the goodness of God and His words was to worship Him right then right there, in the artistic expression of his sacrifice.

During this time period many built altars, but the main point here is that Worship 2.0 consisted primarily of offering sacrifices unto God, a practice that would continue until the offering of the ultimate sacrifice of God's son. This act would end the need for all sacrifices.

Worship 2.0 continued up until the time of Exodus 25, when Moses received instructions on how to build the Tabernacle. At that point, an elaborate Tabernacle was in place, along with the associated ritual, and the formation of the Levitical ministry to tend to the Tabernacle, and later the Temple, and to the acts of worship themselves.

KEY ASPECT: Introduction of more formalized rituals and offerings.

Worship 3.0

This time period is what we would consider the worship during the Mosaic Law. Worship 3.0 was the worship that was in place as David began to walk in his calling, fulfilling his purposes in God. Just prior to David, worship was centered at the Tabernacle at Gibeon, maintained until Solomon built his Temple in Jerusalem.

> The king went to Gibeon to sacrifice there, for that was the great high place; Solomon offered a thousand burnt offerings on that altar." (1 Kings 3:4).

God's presence was found at the Ark of the Covenant, the central and innermost part of the temple and tabernacle. There is a ton of history to study regarding the tabernacle and temple of this time. For our purposes, we'll have a brief look at how this worship might apply to our consideration of Worship 4.0.

The tabernacle was established by Moses in Worship 3.0, recorded in Exodus chapters 25 and following. The Ark of the Covenant was built in this time period, and was intended to host the presence of God. It was where God was to dwell among His people.

> And there I will meet with the children of Israel, and the tabernacle shall be sanctified by my glory.
>
> And I will sanctify the tabernacle of the congregation, and the altar: I will sanctify also both Aaron and his sons, to minister to me in the priest's office.
>
> And I will dwell among the children of Israel, and will be their God. (Exod. 29:43-45)

Aaron and all the priests were to place a lamp in the tabernacle and maintain it so that it would always burn to signify the presence of God.

> And thou shalt command the children of Israel,
> that they bring thee pure oil olive beaten for the
> light, to cause the lamp to burn always. (Exod.
> 27:20)

Later, the Levites were given the full responsibility of the
tabernacle, both in the physical and in the spiritual. They were
to handle the cleaning, tear down and set up as they moved
from place to place, and all of the ceremony and sacrifices that
were part of worship.

> But appoint the Levites over the tabernacle of the
> testimony, and over all its furnishings, and over all
> that belongs to it. They are to carry the tabernacle
> and all its furnishings, and they shall take care of
> it and shall camp around the tabernacle. (Num.
> 1:50)

The tabernacle was the model for the temple to come. It was
portable and able to be moved as the children of Israel moved
from place to place. But it still had the basic architecture of the
temple to come. There were entry gates, outer courts, inner
courts, and a Holy of Holies that housed the Ark. Both the
tabernacle and the temple foreshadowed our time, where God
would dwell in His people.

> Know ye not that ye are the temple of God, and
> that the Spirit of God dwelleth in you? (1 Cor.
> 3:16)

Here are some thoughts and observations regarding Worship
3.0:

- There were continual animal sacrifices.

  > For since the law has but a shadow of the good
  > things to come instead of the true form of these
  > realities, it can never, by the same sacrifices
  > that are continually offered every year, make
  > perfect those who draw near. (Heb. 10:1)

- Personal worship was noted:

  > And when all the people saw the pillar of cloud standing at the entrance of the tent, all the people would rise up and worship, each at his tent door. (So there was personal worship here to, but pretty much one-way, man to God. (Exod. 33:10)

- Formal community worship was specifically noted in scripture:

  > In the first month in the second year, on the first day of the month, the tabernacle was erected.

  > Moses erected the tabernacle. He laid its bases, and set up its frames, and put in its poles, and raised up its pillars.

  > And he spread the tent over the tabernacle and put the covering of the tent over it, as the LORD had commanded Moses.

  > He took the testimony and put it into the ark, and put the poles on the ark and set the mercy seat above on the ark.

  > And he brought the ark into the tabernacle and set up the veil of the screen, and screened the ark of the testimony, as the LORD had commanded Moses.

  > He put the table in the tent of meeting, on the north side of the tabernacle, outside the veil,

  > and arranged the bread on it before the LORD, as the LORD had commanded Moses.

  > He put the lampstand in the tent of meeting, opposite the table on the south side of the tabernacle,

and set up the lamps before the LORD, as the LORD had commanded Moses.

He put the golden altar in the tent of meeting before the veil,

and burned fragrant incense on it, as the LORD had commanded Moses.

He put in place the screen for the door of the tabernacle.

And he set the altar of burnt offering at the entrance of the tabernacle of the tent of meeting, and offered on it the burnt offering and the grain offering, as the LORD had commanded Moses.

He set the basin between the tent of meeting and the altar, and put water in it for washing,

with which Moses and Aaron and his sons washed their hands and their feet.

When they went into the tent of meeting, and when they approached the altar, they washed, as the LORD commanded Moses.

And he erected the court around the tabernacle and the altar, and set up the screen of the gate of the court. So Moses finished the work.

Then the cloud covered the tent of meeting, and the glory of the LORD filled the tabernacle.

And Moses was not able to enter the tent of meeting because the cloud settled on it, and the glory of the LORD filled the tabernacle.

Throughout all their journeys, whenever the cloud was taken up from over the tabernacle, the people of Israel would set out. (Exod. 40:17-36)

This is also the time period when David brought the Ark of the Covenant into Jerusalem during his reign as king. David instituted a "freer, more expressive" form of worship. There still was the Ark, and the Tabernacle, which evolved quickly into Solomon's Temple, with all the accompanying ritual, sacrifice and formalities. What David brought was free and open musical worship, along with dancing.

> And David danced before the LORD with all his might. And David was wearing a linen ephod.
>
> So David and all the house of Israel brought up the ark of the LORD with shouting and with the sound of the horn.
>
> As the ark of the LORD came into the city of David, Michal the daughter of Saul looked out of the window and saw King David leaping and dancing before the LORD... (2 Sam. 6:14-16)

David is often considered the father of modern worship, as many of us consider worship. Worship was free, uninhibited, with dancing, all sorts of music, and thanksgiving. Worship 3.0 was the given ceremonial worship of the Old Testament. It was the domain of the Levites, with their many rules, laws, days and time. David "opened up" this worship, forming a new generation of worship. As with Worship 2.0, it was more or less one way and representational. Priests still went to God to represent the people before Him.

David also modeled the incorporation of the arts with worship. This is not without precedent, however, as the integration of art in the Tabernacle, and later the Temple, was directed by God and abundantly provided by Israel. In Exodus, God gave Moses the architectural and interior design plans for the Tabernacle. ([7], pg 21)

> And let them make me a sanctuary, that I may dwell in their midst.

> Exactly as I show you concerning the pattern of the tabernacle, and of all its furniture, so you shall make it. (Exod. 25:8, 9)

Art that represented God, and as directed by God, was placed in the very center of this place of worship. ([6], pg 23)

> And you shall make two cherubim of gold; of hammered work shall you make them, on the two ends of the mercy seat. (Exod. 25:18)

> "You shall make a lampstand of pure gold. The lampstand shall be made of hammered work: its base, its stem, its cups, its calyxes, and its flowers shall be of one piece with it.

> And there shall be six branches going out of its sides, three branches of the lampstand out of one side of it and three branches of the lampstand out of the other side of it;

> three cups made like almond blossoms, each with calyx and flower, on one branch, and three cups made like almond blossoms, each with calyx and flower, on the other branch--so for the six branches going out of the lampstand. (Exod. 25:31-33)

Later, Solomon's Temple was adorned with art, both inside and out, that represented the beauty of God and his nature. Again, the plans and designs were provided by God. ([6], pg 25)

> Then David gave Solomon his son the plan of the vestibule of the temple, and of its houses, its treasuries, its upper rooms, and its inner chambers, and of the room for the mercy seat;

> and the plan of all that he had in mind for the courts of the house of the LORD, all the surrounding chambers, the treasuries of the house of God, and the treasuries for dedicated gifts; (1 Chron. 28:11, 12)

"All this he made clear to me in writing from
the hand of the LORD, all the work to be done
according to the plan." (1 Chron. 28:19)

Art was both abundant and extravagant, found in virtually
all parts of the Temple. ([6] pgs 28, 29]

Around all the walls of the house he carved
engraved figures of cherubim and palm trees and
open flowers, in the inner and outer rooms. (1
Kings 6:29)

Music also played a critical part in the worship of David's
time. We see in 1 Chronicles that 4,000 musicians served in
Temple worship. ([6], pgs 40, 41)

4,000 gatekeepers, and 4,000 shall offer praises to
the LORD with the instruments that I have made
for praise." (1 Chron. 23:5)

And he stationed the Levites in the house of the
LORD with cymbals, harps, and lyres, according
to the commandment of David and of Gad the
king's seer and of Nathan the prophet, for the
commandment was from the LORD through his
prophets.

The Levites stood with the instruments of David,
and the priests with the trumpets. (2 Chron.
29:25-26)

Dance was another art form that was used in worship. In
Psalms, dance was mentioned as a form of praise. ([6], pg 45)

Let them praise his name with dancing, making
melody to him with tambourine and lyre! (Psalm
149:3)

Praise him with trumpet sound; praise him with
lute and harp!

Praise him with tambourine and dance; praise him
with strings and pipe!

> Praise him with sounding cymbals; praise him
> with loud clashing cymbals! (Psalm 150:3-5)

Francis A. Schaeffer notes in *Art and the Bible*,

> "... an art work has value as a creation because
> man is made in the image of God, and therefore
> man not only can love and think and feel emotion
> but also has the capacity to create. Being in the
> image of the Creator, we are called upon to have
> creativity. In fact, it is part of the image of God to
> be creative, or to have creativity." ([6], pg 51)

David brought both reclaimed territory and artistic
expression in worship. Moses's Tabernacle, Solomon's Temple,
and the corresponding worship was the genesis of a new, more
expressive type of worship. This worship allowed for the artistic
expression of the worshiper.

Here are some thoughts and observations pertaining to
Worship 3.0.

- As was true for Worship 2.0, Worship 3.0 could be
  considered "one-way" worship; we move to Him.

  > Enter his gates with thanksgiving, and his
  > courts with praise! Give thanks to him; bless
  > his name! (Ps. 100:4)

- They ministered with song before the tabernacle of the
  tent of meeting until Solomon built the house of the
  LORD in Jerusalem, and they performed their service
  according to their order.

  > These are the men whom David put in charge
  > of the service of song in the house of the LORD
  > after the ark rested there. (1 Chron. 6:31,32)

- Added creativity and the arts. Worship outside the tent
  walls, beginning to set the prophetic pattern of that
  which would come with the giving of Holy Spirit.

- This pattern would continue through the Cross.

- Worship 3.0 placed man (by proxy of the high priest) "in heaven" (via proxy of the Holy of Holies).

KEY ASPECT: It was representational, the priests represented man to God. While there are instances of both personal and community worship, it was still required that the priests of the time carry on with very complicated and demanding rituals, culminating each year with the High Priest entering into the presence of God, that is, in the Holy of Holies, to offer sacrifices for the sins of the entire people. Man had to move to God, offering sacrifices for sin.

KEY ASPECT: Continual animal sacrifices, providing a temporary covering for sin (I Kings 3:4, Heb. 10:1).

KEY ASPECT: Worship 3.0 started with a hint, but ended with an abundance of personal expression in music, art, dance, and possibly other expressive forms. David was the turning point as he both captured and restored the physical territory of God's people, but simultaneously introduced expressive worship on a massive scale.

Worship 4.0

So what then is Worship 4.0? I believe it's not a replacement, but a layering, a new way of thinking, a new way of doing things. It's something that is emerging, and can be incorporated into existing worship structures. It is different because it begins inside the individual's heart first, emanating from their spirit. It is God's desire to dwell inside the heart, and rekindle the friendship with mankind He once had. Worship is to be an internal reality with external evidence. Worship 4.0 works from the inside out, not from the outside in.

There are worship warriors emerging as well, that carry a vision of emerging intimacy and power, of growth, expansion, the reclaiming of what is truly God's and God's people. It is a vision that is not of man but of Him, not from the Church, but *for* the Church. It is worship that reclaims and holds territory.

I believe that this territory is one of true identity and purpose. This territory has been given to God's people, but abdicated over time through apathy, fear, embarrassment and disempowerment. Israel took on the identity of inferior victims, ultimately leading to total captivity, being dominated by their enemies. David restored the identity of royalty, of being God's people, strong, free, and blessed. Unless we think of ourselves as God thinks of us, and see our purpose as God sees our purpose, we will never walk in harmony with His purposes for us. In worship, we can take this territory, allowing the Holy Spirit to teach us and guide us into who we really are in Him.

In the Old Testament, the territory was physical, promised to Israel and reclaimed by David. Now, the territory to reclaim is our true identity and purpose before God. Worship 4.0 is more than an expression of bridal love for the King, more than an expression of desperation and more than a retreat into the domain of the King. It's a carrying of that domain into the world, the establishment of "portals of influence" physically here on earth where people can fellowship and receive from Him. Worship 4.0 is an apostolic movement, establishing heaven on earth, which can expand from neighborhoods to cities, and nations.

David modeled the taking of territory along with implementing creative expression in worship. Let's review what David did, and how he accomplished it. As with everything, God is the initiator. God originally promised His people physical territory.

> The LORD said to Abram, after Lot had separated from him, "Lift up your eyes and look from the place where you are, northward and southward and eastward and westward,
>
> for all the land that you see I will give to you and to your offspring forever. (Gen. 13:14-15)
>
> On that day the LORD made a covenant with Abram, saying, "To your offspring I give this land, from the river of Egypt to the great river, the river Euphrates,
>
> the land of the Kenites, the Kenizzites, the Kadmonites,
>
> the Hittites, the Perizzites, the Rephaim,
>
> the Amorites, the Canaanites, the Girgashites and the Jebusites." (Gen. 15:18-21)

However, over time Israel had abdicated its rightful territory, leaving it in the hands of their enemies. The record found in 2 Samuel 8, shows the redemptive record of David's reclamation of the lands God promised to His people. David was a warring man, but all for God, and all to take back territory that rightfully belonged to God's people.

Ultimately, God fulfilled His promise through David, and God blessed His people.

> Thus the LORD gave to Israel all the land that he swore to give to their fathers. And they took possession of it, and they settled there.
>
> And the LORD gave them rest on every side just as he had sworn to their fathers. Not one of all their

enemies had withstood them, for the LORD had given all their enemies into their hands.

Not one word of all the good promises that the LORD had made to the house of Israel had failed; all came to pass. (Josh. 21:43-45)

David's territory was physical, occupied by the enemy, and ultimately reclaimed according to God's promises. I believe our territory is our identity, function, and purpose before God. Our personal identity and concepts of purpose are built over time by what we hear, experience, and ultimately believe about ourselves.

If we hear and believe lies, then we become them, and in a self-fulfilling way, we live them. The narratives that we experience in our family life, school, work, relationships and through the influences of culture become our own identity and purpose. This is the territory that has been taken from us. Our "land of the -ites" is our true identity and purpose, and we must "war" to restore these lands to rightful ownership.

Isaiah 61 gives us a beautiful model of how this is to be done in showing us one of the aspects of the ministry of the coming Savior, the Lord Jesus Christ.

The Spirit of the Lord GOD is upon me, because the LORD has anointed me to bring good news to the poor; he has sent me to bind up the brokenhearted, to proclaim liberty to the captives, and the opening of the prison to those who are bound;

to proclaim the year of the LORD's favor, and the day of vengeance of our God; to comfort all who mourn;

to grant to those who mourn in Zion-- to give them a beautiful headdress instead of ashes, the oil of gladness instead of mourning, the garment of praise instead of a faint spirit; that they may be called oaks of righteousness, the planting of the LORD, that he may be glorified. (Isa. 61:1-3)

The restoration provided here is one of exchange. We are to exchange that which is *not* true with that which *is* true. Note the occurrences of "instead of" in verse three. Through His work and ministry, we are able to replace the bad with the good. In His work, we are empowered to replace the false narratives in our lives with truth.

In the past, our territory of identity and purpose may have been taken and inhabited by lies that are simply not true. Everything we do comes out of our identity: who we think we are, what we think about ourselves, and most importantly, who we think God is to us. Identity is built by our parents, our cultural influences, our friends and other family, our time in school, and from our relationships. It can also be built by a deliberate and intentional effort on our part to discover who we were made to be in Christ. Are we sons, servants, both, broken, or complete? All these can be found in the Bible, and explored in worship.

Our time in worship can be a time of self-discovery as the Holy Spirit teaches us about who we are, and who Jesus is. He wants to help us be more like Jesus, and understand more of how the Father thinks of us. In worship, we can participate in this journey of self-discovery, uninhibited, unfettered, and uncontrolled by others. Often it seems that the express purpose of other people is to tell you who you are, what you can and cannot do, and what you will become. As we identify and replace the untrue, we step more and more into the territory God has for us.

There are many aspects of this "war," and many ways to accomplish this. We can become established and continue to grow in our knowledge of His written Word. We avail ourselves of fellowship with like-minded believers who speak truth into our lives. We associate ourselves with leaders who also minister grace to us, and build true identity and purpose into us and, we can participate in deep and expressive worship of our King and one true God.

Worship 4.0 can play a vital part in the development of our true identity and calling, hence taking territory and holding space for Holy Spirit to work within us to will and to do of His good pleasure.

What David modeled in Worship 3.0, God accomplished in Worship 4.0. The territory of our identity and purpose has been restored through the work of Jesus Christ, and through the in-working of the Holy Spirit. We are now complete in Him in all things, fit for our purpose in service to and with Him.

> And ye are complete in him, which is the head of all principality and power: (Col. 2:10 KJV).

> for it is God who works in you, both to will and to work for his good pleasure. (Phil. 2:13)

> Working together with him, then, we appeal to you not to receive the grace of God in vain. (2 Cor. 6:1)

Like David, Worship 4.0 carries all the power of war, with all the freedom of the arts. Worship 4.0 can connect personal transformation to societal change in bringing Godly solutions to world problems, through worshipful believers in alignment with His purposes in their own callings.

Worship 4.0 started practically with the day of Pentecost, with the giving of the gift of Holy Spirit to all those who asked. With the in-dwelling Holy Spirit created within, God established a habitational culture, moving his Church into a family relationship in addition to the servant relationship. Worship 4.0 took 3.0 through the cross. The veil of separation between God and man was torn down, ripped from top to bottom, symbolizing man's free and unfettered access to God.

> Let us then with confidence draw near to the throne of grace, that we may receive mercy and find grace to help in time of need. (Heb. 4:16)

Man's worship was no longer "representational," but direct and personal. Worship 4.0 is now emerging through an explosion in artistic worship and personal relationship with God, with freedom of expression and the artistic representation of heaven.

One great aspect of Worship 4.0 is that it can be a heavenly "portal" here on earth. Instead of the "earth-to-heaven" one-way model, it brings a "heaven-to-earth" model, establishing a Kingdom environment on earth in worship.

This portal concept is illustrated in Genesis 28 and begins when Jacob has a dream.

> And he dreamed, and behold, there was a ladder set up on the earth, and the top of it reached to heaven. And behold, the angels of God were ascending and descending on it!
>
> And behold, the LORD stood above it and said, "I am the LORD, the God of Abraham your father and the God of Isaac. The land on which you lie I will give to you and to your offspring.
>
> Your offspring shall be like the dust of the earth, and you shall spread abroad to the west and to the east and to the north and to the south, and in you and your offspring shall all the families of the earth be blessed.
>
> Behold, I am with you and will keep you wherever you go, and will bring you back to this land. For I will not leave you until I have done what I have promised you."
>
> Then Jacob awoke from his sleep and said, "Surely the LORD is in this place, and I did not know it."
>
> And he was afraid and said, "How awesome is this place! This is none other than the house of God, and this is the gate of heaven." (Gen. 28:12-17)

As shown in the *Power of Sound* chapter of this book, here is an example of Saul literally stepping into a godly atmosphere (or portal) on earth, and being changed by it.

> After that you shall come to Gibeath-elohim, where there is a garrison of the Philistines. And there, as soon as you come to the city, you will

meet a group of prophets coming down from the high place with harp, tambourine, flute, and lyre before them, prophesying.

Then the Spirit of the LORD will rush upon you, and you will prophesy with them and be turned into another man.

Now when these signs meet you, do what your hand finds to do, for God is with you.

When he turned his back to leave Samuel, God gave him another heart. And all these signs came to pass that day. (1 Sam. 10:5-9)

This example shows where both Saul and his messengers are affected by this portal of heaven on earth. Here is a different incident showing the same concept.

Then Saul sent messengers to take David, and when they saw the company of the prophets prophesying, and Samuel standing as head over them, the Spirit of God came upon the messengers of Saul, and they also prophesied.

When it was told Saul, he sent other messengers, and they also prophesied. And Saul sent messengers again the third time, and they also prophesied.

Then he himself went to Ramah and came to the great well that is in Secu. And he asked, "Where are Samuel and David?" And one said, "Behold, they are at Naioth in Ramah."

And he went there to Naioth in Ramah. And the Spirit of God came upon him also, and as he went he prophesied until he came to Naioth in Ramah. (1 Sam. 19:20-23)

Worship 4.0 is more of a "two-way" concept, where in addition to offering our thanksgiving and praises to God, He in turn comes and works with us. The worshipers of today, both musical and otherwise, partner with Holy Spirit to establish an environment that will host His presence more evidently. We "take territory" and "hold space" for the Holy Spirit to move within His people, and do whatever He wants. The worship team partners with the Holy Spirit to do what He wants to do in these worship times. Worship 4.0 teams take territory (with music, art, dance, and other expressive arts) and hold space for the Holy Spirit to do the leading. They are to be spiritually sensitive to move with Him where He wants to go.

KEY ASPECT: The Holy Spirit becomes the worship leader, and we partner with Him.

> When the Spirit of truth comes, He will guide you into all truth. He will not speak on His own but will tell you what He has heard. He will tell you about the future. (John 16:13)

KEY ASPECT: There is no longer a need for special priests to represent man to God.

> And you will be My kingdom of priests, My holy nation. This is the message you must give to the people of Israel." (Exod. 19:6)

> They will rebuild the ancient ruins, repairing cities destroyed long ago. They will revive them, though they have been deserted for many Generations. (Isa. 61:4)

> But you are not like that, for you are a chosen people. You are royal priests, a holy nation, God's very own possession. As a result, you can show others the goodness of God, for He called you out of the darkness into His wonderful light. (1 Pet. 2:9)

We are all now to be priests, and to participate in the rebuilding and revival spoken of in Isaiah 61:4. I believe that Worship 4.0 can be part of the rebuilding of the ancient ruins of true worship.

KEY ASPECT: Relationship as a beloved son or daughter is celebrated and practiced. It's all about relationship, and Worship 4.0 celebrates and soaks in that relationship. It's a *two*-way, direct relationship now.

KEY ASPECT: We declare and live the identity that Christ gave His life for, in worship. We are righteous now, cleansed, forgiven, made strong in Him. We can understand God who is for us, and live in His peace. There is so much more, but these are the kinds of concepts we celebrate in song with Worship 4.0. [9]

KEY ASPECT: We move from pursuing His presence to practicing it.

A Shift in Mindsets

We have seen that Worship 4.0 has introduced a number of concepts yet emerging in our worship culture. Among these are freedom of expression, relationship in worship, and a communing with the heavenly Father. But perhaps all of these are contained in one simple mindset, that worship is a creative process, and as such, flows from the creative mind. But what is the "creative mind," and how do we engage it in creative worship, Worship 4.0?

Let's explore the concepts of left-sided and right-sided thinking, but please understand it is not our purpose to present one as "better" than the other, or try to reduce one to promote the other. What we want to bring is that the full function of the whole brain, as God built it and intended it to work, involves *both* parts, the left and the right.

The Bible offers a superb example of this in the account of Mary and Martha, but let's first consider the left-right concept. It's commonly understood that our brains are actually two, almost completely separated, "pieces," connected by a broad band of nerve fibers called the corpus callosum. The "whole" brain actually consists of two very distinct sections, each with very distinct characteristics and functionalities.

The "Left Side":

The left side is the rational, logical side. We often think of this one as the "thinking" side. This where planning takes place, and our sense of time resides. It is linear and task-oriented, concerned with outcomes and production. The left side is always considering what needs to be done next, or what has been done in the past. It seems to always be planning or learning, living in the future or in the past, but rarely in the moment of now. It is here where logic and reason reign supreme, living in the world of time, planning, words and numbers.

Both language and math are linear, moving from one thought to the next, in a very structured and controlled fashion. Things in left-mode thinking "make sense," they are logical, and rational. A burning bush that talks to us, for example, does not "make sense," it's not "possible," and doesn't fit in left-mode thinking. The left mode deals in the realm of what is possible, and how it can be accomplished. Left-mode thinking is the "doing" side of life, expecting determined results through planning and structure.

The "Right Side":

The right side is where creativity and imagination lie. It is where intuition flourishes, with no sense of whether it makes sense or if it will work. Dreams and callings are found in right-mode thinking, and faith is found there, as there is no concern of whether something is possible. We become born again by believing the impossible, that God raised Jesus from the dead to forever live at His right hand. That's impossible, at least to the left mode of thinking. It doesn't make sense, it's not logical or rational. There are so many things about the nature of God that are not strictly logical or rational. Donkeys talk, axe heads float in water, bushes burn and talk, men walk on water, blind are made to see, dead are made alive, and people are healed of impossible diseases.

Right-mode thinking embraces the impossible, and actually revels in it! Right-mode thinking is circular, and moves around and over and through, often with no particular purpose, direction or structure. Whereas the left mode is primarily concerned with the past and the future, the right side lives in the moment, and is easily lost in time, with little concern with the future. It is the "being" part of life, not so much the planning part. Right-mode thinking is relational, looking for connection, fellowship, and simply abiding in the present time.

Both Together:

God's miracle of creation, and the purpose of man, emerges when *both* sides work together. They each provide complementary, not competing, functionality. Creative writing involves both modes, as does music. Teaching styles are being developed that appeal and communicate to both sides of the brain. Left-mode thinking can bring understanding and intentionality to the dreams and callings found in the right side. Creativity is fostered in the right side, and faith abounds in right-mode thinking. Correspondingly, the left side brings our understanding of God's written Word, and all the truth it provides.

Creativity without truth will not provide a heavenly atmosphere on earth. But neither will accomplishing tasks without inspired creative direction, regardless of our own logic and reason. Knowledge of God without corresponding experience is hollow, and a mental exercise at best. But supernatural experience without the knowledge of God can easily be counterfeit and destructive. In order to live and worship, we need both modes of thinking, applied at the appropriate times, as God directs and Holy Spirit moves.

Worship 4.0 is designed to engage the creative mind, foster faith, develop dreams and destiny, and clarify callings. The practical aspect of applying Worship 4.0 concepts to a worship service requires a shift in thinking, from primarily left-mode to primarily right-mode, as illustrated by Mary and Martha and their evening with Jesus. It's a short and poignant account found in the Gospel of Luke that will offer insight to our approach to worship, both personally and corporately.

Many people have taught and wrote on this section, but please simply consider its lessons in light of the rational and creative modes of thinking we have been exploring and how they may apply to worship. Following are several versions of this account, which I believe will be interesting to consider. First, the English Standard Version:

> Now as they went on their way, Jesus entered a village. And a woman named Martha welcomed him into her house. And she had a sister called

Mary, who sat at the Lord's feet and listened to his teaching. But Martha was distracted with much serving. And she went up to him and said, "Lord, do you not care that my sister has left me to serve alone? Tell her then to help me."But the Lord answered her, "Martha, Martha, you are anxious and troubled about many things,but one thing is necessary. Mary has chosen the good portion, which will not be taken away from her." (Luke 10:38-42)

(The Amplified Version) Now while they were on their way, it occurred that Jesus entered a certain village, and a woman named Martha received and welcomed Him into her house. And she had a sister named Mary, who seated herself at the Lord's feet and was listening to His teaching. But Martha [*overly occupied and too busy*] was distracted with much serving; and she came up to Him and said, Lord, is it nothing to You that my sister has left me to serve alone? Tell her then to help me [*to lend a hand and do her part along with me*]! But the Lord replied to her by saying, Martha, Martha, you are anxious and troubled about many things; There is need of only one or but a few things. Mary has chosen the good portion [*that which is to her advantage*], which shall not be taken away from her. (Luke 10:38-42)

(The Message Bible) As they continued their travel, Jesus entered a village. A woman by the name of Martha welcomed him and made him feel quite at home. She had a sister, Mary, who sat before the Master, hanging on every word he said. But Martha was pulled away by all she had to do in the kitchen. Later, she stepped in, interrupting them. "Master, don't you care that my sister has abandoned the kitchen to me? Tell her to lend me a hand." The Master said, "Martha, dear Martha, you're fussing far too much and getting yourself worked up over nothing. One thing only is essential, and Mary has chosen it—it's the main course, and won't be taken from her." (Luke 10:38-42)

I'm sure you get the idea here, two different people spending an evening with the Lord. Let's consider this in light of the left and right mode styles of thinking, with admittedly just a "little bit" of conjecture. Martha was very much concerned about the "doing" that she determined to be necessary due to the presence of the Lord. This would be left-mode thinking, looking at all that needed to be done, cleaning the house, preparing appetizers and later dinner, and so on. Certainly, these things were important, and needed to be done, right? Mary on the other hand chose to sit at the feet of Jesus, listening, "hanging on every word" according to the Message version. Mary was in "being" mode, a characteristic of the creative right side. Mary wasn't concerned about the tasks that needed doing, was not caught up in planning the evening, or even helping with the production. She was simply living in the moment, and that moment was at the feet of the Lord, listening, and being with Him. Mary was celebrating her access and relationship with the Lord at that point in time.

So, who was right and who was wrong? I submit that is the wrong question. Rather, who was aligned with His purposes at the moment? I am sure that the "things" and "tasks" that Martha was concerned about were valid, and probably by all rational thinking, needed to be done. But was it what *He* wanted her to be doing? As Jesus Himself modelled for us, He only spoke what He heard the Father say, and only did what He saw the Father doing. Are we to act any differently? This account would appear to say "no." We are to do what He wants us to be doing in the moment, and be who He has called us to be.

In this account, it is somewhat painfully clear that Mary was in the "right" place with Jesus, and Martha was not. Martha was overly concerned, distracted, anxious, troubled, and all worked up. She even found herself accusing the Lord of not caring about her and her tasks! But Jesus' answer to her was so loving, kind, and clear. Mary had chosen the better action, that which was best for the moment, all "production" and "tasks" aside. Mary's choice to simply *be* with the Lord in relationship rather than service was, at this time, the better, more beneficial option, and was where Jesus wanted them both to be. Does that mean that the things that Martha wanted to accomplish were wrong? I don't believe so, but they were lower in priority.

The example of left and right mode types of thinking is very clear. Jesus wanted to abide with them in a right side style of thinking. He wanted to enjoy *being* with them, not just being served by them.

Likewise, Worship 4.0 is all about the being, and holding space, providing the environment so that others can enjoy their relationship with the Lord in the moment as well. This may require a shift in mindsets in how we approach and provide worship in our own lives, and in the churches in which we serve. We'll consider the "how" of bringing this to our worship times and worship services in the next chapter.

The Practice of
Worship 4.0

Incorporating Worship 4.0 into an existing worship atmosphere will take deliberate effort in bringing both the worshippers and the worship team along in Worship 4.0 thinking. Instruction for both should follow a parallel path of mutual learning and growing in this worship culture. Following are a number of practical thoughts, both for worshipers and worship teams. Although these keys are in no particular order, I would submit that a worship team member would need to be in the "as worshipers" place before moving into the additional responsibility of the worship team. The worship team musician is no different than the vocalist worship "leader" in that regard. We all participate equally in hosting the presence of God, and setting the atmosphere of heaven.

As worshipers, our job is:

- To view worship time as being home with the Father. This should not be a time of (our own) work, rather, resting in His work, fellowshiping with Him.

- A personal time, to encounter Him.

- A time to *be* with Him, be His beloved, allowing Him to lavish His love upon us, responding with all praise, thanksgiving, and love for Him.

- To offer our walk of love as sacrifice (Ephesians 5:2). Without this *first*, all the subsequent actions, (raising hands, voices, shouting, singing) are hollow and considered "noise" (1 Corinthians 13: 1-3). He desires compassion above sacrifice (Matthew 9:13).

- To worship within the *love* context, warm affection and honor for one another.

As a worship team, our job is:

- To be in the right place yourself! (See above.)
- To provide the environment of heaven to host Him, which is our apostolic function.
- To design the worship time and service to foster and engage the right mode of thinking, and provide that shift.
  - Consider the worship time to be its own time, not so much just preparation for the message.
  - Plan a block of several songs to allow for fifteen to twenty minutes of uninterrupted fellowship with the Lord, and give Holy Spirit time to show people what He wants to show them by allowing people time to settle in with Him. (Some churches allow an hour of relatively uninterrupted worship!)
  - As leaders, honor His time with His people, and only do what He wants us to do during the service. Choose His priorities, not ours.
  - This one might take some growing into, but allow for space and freedom for people to walk around, pray with and for people, perhaps a "river" at the front for deep (community) worship together.
- To take the territory of the room. (Our authority in Him through our music.) Areas include:
  - Identity
  - Rest
  - Relationship
  - Creativity
  - Emotions
- To partner with the Holy Spirit with Him as the worship leader.
- To not get in His way! *He* is the Comforter, Teacher, and Guide. (That's His job!) In short, don't try to do His job.

- To not distract the people from their time with Him.

- To be sensitive to Him and what He is working in the people, then work together to host that presence. (i.e., exhortation from the stage, "raise your hands, lift up your voice," and so on. Let it be organic, not legislated. Follow His lead.)

- To hold space and time for Holy Spirit to touch *each* person individually. He wants to do something for *each and every* person.

Other considerations:

- Come into worship carrying the sacrifice of Christ, counting the old man dead, walking in the new man in spirit and in truth.

- Worship within the accomplishments of His sacrifice.

- Know God initiates and we respond (1 John 4:19).

- Let worship be a time of relationship, communication, receiving from Him.

- Think rest, not results, and presence, not performance.

- Stress is introduced when the expectation of a desired result becomes more important than rest and peace. It is never beneficial to add stress into the mix. It causes more problems than benefit. Stress and anxiety can be eliminated when a concerted effort is exerted for peace and rest. Here are some steps toward stress-free worship:

  o Look at God only. Focus on His attitude of divine unconditional love for you.

  o Realize there is no way to earn any more love from Him. There is nothing we can do on our own to "earn" more love from Him, and no amount of negative action or words will cause Him to remove His love from you. God doesn't give His love as a reward for good behavior. Divine love extends beyond human reasoning. It can only be accepted when you realize that it is completely illogical.

o   Once unconditional love is realized and accepted in a heart, then peace can soak in, flood in, and move in. Peace and rest are a result of the knowledge and acceptance of unconditional love (1 Pet. 5:7).

Selecting Worship 4.0 Songs

Following are considerations when selecting songs that will carry the Worship 4.0 heart.

1.   Two-way action (relationship)

2.   New man identity, evokes new man feelings

3.   Encourage, exhort, comfort, edify

4.   Atmosphere – entertainment verses hosting presence

5.   Utilizes "right-side" thinking, i.e., metaphors, visual language

6.   Future-present thinking (destiny, purpose, calling)

7.   The goodness of God

Providing an Atmosphere of Heaven

As a worship team, we work together to not only deliver a song with skill, which is indeed necessary, but perhaps more importantly, we do it with the right heart. As a team, we are to provide an atmosphere of heaven. Here's how I think of working together as a team in this fashion.

Think of a waterfall, with a river flowing from it. If you have ever visited Burney Falls, just an hour outside of Redding,

California, you will know what I mean! If you haven't ever been there, it's worth a visit to sit and consider worship as a river. One thing you could do right now is find a recording of a river or waterfall on YouTube, and listen to that.

As you sit, consider the sound that you are enveloped within. Just the sound. Close your eyes and listen. You'll hear quite a variety of sounds. There will be low rumble sounds, sort of mid-range flowing sounds, and high pitched splashes every now and then that will punctuate the overall sound. Think of a worship band in that way, as a whole "sound" with individual components. Let the bass and drums carry the "beat" of the waterfall, that deep flow of the river that is omnipresent, in all things. Maybe the keys and guitars are the flowing rapids, sitting on top of the rumble, but adding flavor and character to the environment. Then the vocals or lead instruments can bring the sparkle on top of the flow, contributing to the whole sound of the river, the awesome majesty of the waterfall.

Furthermore, let that atmosphere be the atmosphere of heaven. If it's not in heaven, it's not to be in our worship service. Think of the emotions of the song, and of your heart, and let them be the atmosphere of heaven as well. Bring all things into subjection to the King and His kingdom. This is the apostolic nature of music, that when He comes, he is comfortable in His own atmosphere of His own kingdom.

The Lifestyle of Worship

Above all, and through all of this, Worship 4.0 is a lifestyle, not just something we do here and there. Worship is living every breath in agreement and alignment with God in relationship with Him. It's being a living and walking example of heaven on earth. This is how man was intended to live, and how he was originally created. Recall that in the garden, with Adam and Eve, there was no "worship" mentioned. Perhaps that was because worship in the garden was a lifestyle and a direct, intimate relationship. They simply walked with Him in the cool of the day. Their worship was a living, breathing relationship with God and none other. Their lives were worship to Him. We find access to this level of living once again given to mankind with the coming of the gift of Holy Spirit, when man could become once again a whole person of body, soul and spirit, reconciled completely to God. [8]

> And he made from one man every nation of mankind to live on all the face of the earth, having determined allotted periods and the boundaries of their dwelling place,
>
> that they should seek God, in the hope that they might feel their way toward him and find him. Yet he is actually not far from each one of us,
>
> for "'In him we live and move and have our being'; as even some of your own poets have said, "'For we are indeed his offspring.' (Acts 17:26-28)

Worship 4.0 is living with and for Him in everything we do. Whether we are involved with our home life, family, work, play, or church, we do all in relationship with Him, never straying, aligned with His purposes and will for us. In a very real sense, we carry a sphere of heaven around us. And when people come into our sphere, they can experience a bit of heaven, a bit of the atmosphere of heaven. In your sphere, they can feel how God thinks, and be treated how God would treat them. Living in this way *is* worship. Worship is to be a state of *being*, not just a state of doing, and true worship is found in a full and complete relationship with God.

In considering worship as a lifestyle, we can see three different ways God is present with His people in scripture. First, and primarily, we have God's presence within, received when we become born again of His Spirit.

> To them God chose to make known how great among the gentiles are the riches of the glory of this mystery, which is Christ in you, the hope of glory. (Col. 1:27)

> In him you also are being built together into a dwelling place for God by the Spirit. (Eph. 2:22)

This is where we start in considering worship as a lifestyle, that is, your personal relationship with God at any moment in time. It's that secret place that only you and Him share, regardless of the situation, circumstances, or surroundings. Nothing can intrude on you there, for He protects and cherishes that time with you.

The next level of presence we see in the Bible is the "few together" presence spoken of in Matthew.

> Again I say to you, if two of you agree on earth about anything they ask, it will be done for them by my Father in heaven.

> For where two or three are gathered in my name, there am I among them. (Matt. 18:19-20)

This level of presence would be any small group of people gathered together for a godly purpose or function.

The final level of presence we can see is at the macro level, the level of the one body, the church of Christ.

> So then you are no longer strangers and aliens, but you are fellow citizens with the saints and members of the household of God, built on the foundation of the apostles and prophets, Christ

Jesus himself being the cornerstone, in whom the whole structure, being joined together, grows into a holy temple in the Lord.

In him you also are being built together into a dwelling place for God by the Spirit. (Eph. 2:19-22)

Now you are the body of Christ and individually members of it. (1 Cor. 12:27)

Here we find His presence as Head of the one body, our Lord.

Living with worship as a lifestyle involves all three levels of His presence, as we are to be sensitive to His Spirit to host His presence in any of these levels, to the extent and manifestation He would have at that moment.

We can also see the development of worship in the sacrifice(s) we are asked to offer now, in the Worship 4.0 era.

Through him then let us continually offer up a sacrifice of praise to God, that is, the fruit of lips that acknowledge his name. (Heb. 13:15)

I appeal to you therefore, brothers, by the mercies of God, to present your bodies as a living sacrifice, holy and acceptable to God, which is your spiritual worship. (Rom. 12:1)

Our sacrifice today is so much more than animal sacrifices. That which these sacrifices were intended to cover has now been paid for in full by the work of Jesus Christ, and our sacrifice now is of a full and complete lifestyle of praise, living in His light, and our walk of love. Truly our sacrifice, our worship, is to be a lifestyle, lived in, through, and because of Him.

For "'In him we live and move and have our being'; as even some of your own poets have said, "'For we are indeed his offspring.' (Acts 17:28)

Worship 4.0 offers a framework for understanding to begin to develop His presence in our lives on all three levels. As we build our personal relationship of Christ within, and are able to abide therein in any circumstance, any surrounding, we are more and more able to expand our sphere of heavenly influence into small groups or macro-church groups. As Worship 4.0 is applied to our community Church worship, people can find a safe place to be with our Father, and express back to Him the love He first lavished on us. It's our expression and our communion with Him that builds our lifestyle of worship.

True worship comes from the heart of the one who loves to be at home with Him. Those who cherish His indwelling presence will be those who live a lifestyle of worship. It's a life of co-creative partnership with Him, to accomplish His will in our lives. He SO wants to be with you, and for you to be with Him, in everything that you do. Let this relationship emerge in your life so that He is glorified, and His kingdom culture is made known.

Thank you for journeying with me through this view of worship, and I pray all the best for you in your personal worship life with Him.

Endnotes

[1] Two sources were also utilized in the study of the original meaning of "apostolos," or apostle.

Applicable excerpts of both are presented here.

William E. Wenstrom, Jr. Bible Ministries, "Apostolos," https://www.wenstrom.org/downloads/written/word_studies/greek/apostolos.pdf, c2002. Accessed January 20, 2017.

Excerpt:

B. Classical Usage

B.2. It was used for admiral or general officer chosen by the consul to command a fleet or to command an army in a military expedition (generally against Sparta in the Peloponnesian Wars).

B.3. It was also used for a very unusual person who is chosen to command a band of Greek colonists in order to establish a settlement in some other part of the world (Corsica, Italy, Sicily, Western Turkey, Black Sea)

B.9. The noun apostolos is first found in maritime language since the Greeks were a seafaring people and it was also used of military expeditions.

B.10. It would used by the Greeks to designate a cargo ship, a freighter, transport ship, or the fleet sent out (Demosthones).

B.11. Later it denoted a commander of a naval expedition, or a band of colonists sent overseas.

B.20. Liddel and Scott list the following classical meanings for the word (page 220): a. messenger, ambassador, envoy b. commander of a naval force c. naval squadron or expedition d. colony e. packet, order for dispatch f. export license g. cargo dispatched by order

Don Enevoldsen, "Apostolos," http://counterthought.org/apostolos/, April 28, 2012.

Exerpt:

Apostolos in ancient Greece was a nautical term, describing a freighter or a naval force. Over time, the meaning focused on a naval force sent out with a specific mission, and eventually narrowed to the leader of the expedition who was an envoy representing the nation. The Romans used the word in this sense. The New Testament use of the word borrows the idea of envoy or representative, but adds nuances from a related Hebrew word.

The idea of representation was especially prominent in the Jewish use of apostolos at the time. The Hebrew word sheluah referred to a person commissioned with specific tasks, with the emphasis on authorization. This term represented the person who was sent forth by the patriarch at certain times each year to collect silver and gold from various synagogues. Called apostoloi in Greek, representatives of the Jewish rulers were sent to collect the half-shekel tax for the Temple.

[2] E.W. Bullingers, *Figures of Speech Used in the Bible* (Grand Rapids, Michigan: Baker Book House, 1968), 664-665.

[3] There are two sources and excerpts referenced here; one citing a report on the decline in children's creativity, and the report source itself.

Peter Gray, PhD, "As Children's Freedom has Declined, So Has Their Creativity," *Psychology Today* Posted September 17, 2012.

It is sobering, therefore, to read Kyung Hee Kim's recent research report documenting a continuous decline in creativity among American schoolchildren over the last two or three decades.

Kim, who is a professor of education at the College of William and Mary, analyzed scores on a battery of measures of creativity—called the Torrance Tests of Creative Thinking (TTCT)—collected from normative samples of schoolchildren in kindergarten through twelfth grade over several decades. According to Kim's analyses, the scores on these tests at all grade levels began to decline somewhere between 1984 and 1990 and have continued to decline ever since. The drops in scores are highly significant statistically and in some cases very large. In Kim's words, the data indicate that "children have become less emotionally expressive, less energetic, less talkative and verbally expressive, less humorous, less imaginative, less unconventional, less lively and passionate, less perceptive, less apt to connect seemingly irrelevant things, less synthesizing, and less likely to see things from a different angle."

Kyung Hee Kim, "The Creativity Crisis: The Decrease in Creative Thinking Scores on the Torrance Tests of Creative Thinking," *Creativity Research Journal*, pages 285-295, published online: November 9, 2011, Volume 23, 2011, Issue 4.

https://www.psychologytoday.com/blog/freedom-learn/201209/children-s-freedom-has-declined-so-has-their-creativity

ABSTRACT:

The *Torrance Tests of Creative Thinking* (**TTCT**) was developed in 1966 and renormed five times: in 1974, 1984, 1990, 1998, and 2008. The total sample for all six normative samples included 272,599 kindergarten through 12th grade students and adults. Analysis of the normative data showed that creative thinking scores remained static or decreased, starting at sixth grade. Results also indicated that since 1990, even as IQ scores have risen, creative thinking scores have significantly decreased. The decrease for kindergartners through third graders was the most significant.

http://www.tandfonline.com/doi/full/10.1080/10400419.2011.627805?scroll=top&needAccess=true

[4] There are many drawings and sketches of the temple through time, all bearing the same general shape and architecture of the gates, courts, temple, and Holy of Holies. We have used the following:

"Locating Solomon's Temple," Norma Robertson, accessed April 15, 2017. http://templemountlocation.com/chapterOne.html.

[5] Jeff A Benner, *"The Ancient Hebrew Lexicon of the Bible,"* e-Sword software version.

[6] Chau Tu. *"Seeing the Patterns in Sound,"* Sciencefriday.com. November 7, 2016. Accessed May 13, 2017.

[7] Francis A. Schaeffer, "Art and the Bible," IVP Books, 1973, pages as noted.

[8] Refernces for "we are righteous, cleansed, fogiven, and made strong.

We are righteous now.

For as by the one man's disobedience the many were made sinners, so by the one man's obedience the many will be made righteous. (Rom. 5:19)

We are cleansed in Him.

Otherwise, would they not have ceased to be offered, since the worshipers, having once been cleansed, would no longer have any consciousness of sins?

We are forgiven.

And you, who were dead in your trespasses and the uncircumcision of your flesh, God made alive together with him, having forgiven us all our trespasses, (Col. 2:13)

We are made strong.

Finally, be strong in the Lord and in the strength of his might. (Eph. 6:10)

[9] We receive Holy Spirit when we are born again, and through that, are reconciled to God.

But just as at that time he who was born according to the flesh persecuted him who was born according to the Spirit, so also it is now. (Gal 4:29)

Since you have been born again, not of perishable seed but of imperishable, through the living and abiding word of God; (1 Pet. 1:23)

Everyone who believes that Jesus is the Christ has been born of God, and everyone who loves the Father loves whoever has been born of him. (1 John 5:1)

And ye are complete in him, which is the head of all principality and power: (Col. 2:10)

Made in the USA
San Bernardino, CA
23 July 2017